Enlightening Encounters

# Enlightening Encounters

## *The Journeys of an Anthropologist*

Stephen Gudeman

berghahn
NEW YORK • OXFORD
www.berghahnbooks.com

First published in 2023 by
Berghahn Books
www.berghahnbooks.com



**Library of Congress Cataloging-in-Publication Data**

Names: Gudeman, Stephen, author.
Title: Enlightening Encounters: The Journeys of an Anthropologist / Stephen Gudeman.
Description: New York: Berghahn Books, 2023. | Includes bibliographical references and index. | Contents: The Road to Anthropology — The Two Cambridges — Panama and an Interlude — Life and Text Together — Colombia — Excursions.
Identifiers: LCCN 2022027934 (print) | LCCN 2022027935 (ebook) | ISBN 9781800736047 (hardback) | ISBN 9781800736061 (paperback) | ISBN 9781800736054 (ebook)
Subjects: LCSH: Gudeman, Stephen F. | Ethnology—Fieldwork. | Ethnology—Latin America. | Anthropologists—United States—Biography
Classification: LCC GN21.G766 A3 2023 (print) | LCC GN21.G766 (ebook) | DDC 305.80092 [B]—dc23/eng/20220719
LC record available at https://lccn.loc.gov/2022027934
LC ebook record available at https://lccn.loc.gov/2022027935

**British Library Cataloguing in Publication Data**

A catalogue record for this book is available from the British Library

ISBN 978-1-80073-604-7 hardback
ISBN 978-1-80073-606-1 paperback
ISBN 978-1-80073-605-4 ebook

https://doi.org/10.3167/9781800736047

# Contents

# Preface

My journey in anthropology began in the summer after my junior year in college when I lived in a small Indigenous village in southern Mexico. Unready for the experience, I accomplished little during those months but watched the people grow and cook the food they shared with me. I doubted that I could survive in their remote and difficult circumstances or succeed as an anthropologist.

Five years later I lived with my wife, Roxane, in lowland Panama where we spent a year and a half immersed in the life of a small village. Now I was trained in anthropology and business and was being supported to devise ways of enhancing rural development, prepare teaching materials for students of business, and undertake research for a PhD. From the first days of our arrival, I turned from analyzing the people's economy using methods I had learned in business school to exploring local life as a field anthropologist. I started with the villagers' economy centered around the house and soon expanded to their social and ritual practices, while I formed a grim view of their welfare and local environment.

A decade after the fieldwork in Panama, when I had a secure academic position, Roxane was teaching at a nearby college, and our three children were in school, I turned to highland Colombia and to collaborative fieldwork with a former student. I found that a people's way of conceiving economy may come from their ideas about the human body, the house, how the world has been made, and their religious beliefs. Economic life is often formulated through such images and metaphors, a perspective I had already used to understand some Western ideas about economy.

Then, shifting from rural economies to the periphery of urban markets in Guatemala, I considered how a house economy becomes a house-business and earns a small profit. What had been a product of making do in the house can become an innovation for sales.

After studying rural economies and their connection to urban markets, as well as histories of markets and market theory, I turned briefly to Cuba to see how a socialist economy operates at the house level and compare it to my prior studies.

Shortly after this journey, I directed a research team undertaking a comparative study in six former socialist countries of Eastern Europe. We found a revival of the house economy after the socialist framework collapsed as well as a resurgence of rituals that support it. Many of the local economic practices in this historically distant place were recognizable to me from my prior journeys in Latin America.

From the first days of fieldwork, my aim was to develop a theoretical perspective for analyzing economy. I do not emphasize that part of the journey, which mostly took place away from the field, but the intention is implicit in what I did while doing the fieldwork and a few of those conclusions are woven into the text.

Throughout the journey, I interacted with many anthropologists and other social scientists who expanded my thinking, and I was fortunate to have university colleagues and students who supported me as well. With my thanks to them for many conversations and written communications, those parts of the journey are not described in order to focus on the anthropology I pursued in the field.

The text, arranged by the flow of time, is divided into five titled chapters. To preserve their anonymity, I have changed the names and features of the people I met during fieldwork but known figures are presented as I saw them.

Growing up, I learned about making do when my family was putting together a dinner from leftovers or I was constructing something with my father. In fieldwork, I saw people making do as they worked in the fields, repaired a tool, assembled a meal, or made something for sale. Much later, I realized that making do captures some of my fieldwork practices and their presentation in this book.

CHAPTER 1

# The Road to Anthropology

One Sunday afternoon in the early 1950s, my dad's cousin came for a visit to our suburban house north of Chicago. I had just entered my teen years, and seeing an opportunity to escape homework, I joined them in our living room. Dad's cousin was seated at one end of our couch. Dad sat upright in a chair with wooden arms to his left. I settled into a cushioned armchair to Dad's left.

Dad was telling his cousin about his job overseeing Sears Roebuck buyers, working with suppliers, controlling inventory and distribution through the stores, and watching the economy to anticipate consumer spending. He knew how much people spent from their income and the competition Sears faced for that portion of their spending. He took pleasure in bringing quality goods at reasonable prices to customers. I had often heard about this part of his job. Then he discussed how Sears, one of the largest corporations in the world at the time, was expanding to places outside the United States. The company had just opened stores in Mexico and parts of South America. Now, it was looking further afield.

I had been mentally dozing until I suddenly sat up to ask, "Why are you trying to expand? Doesn't growth reach an end? Don't you run out of places?"

He replied, "There are many places to go, such as Australia and England."

"What's the purpose?" I asked.

"We want to increase sales," he said

"But why is that important?" I queried.

"We'll bring goods to more people at good prices," he answered.

I had heard this response many times but was not convinced about the urgency of growth, and the two of us went back and forth.

"Can't you be satisfied with what you have?" I asked.

"If we don't expand, others will take our place and our possible profits."

Dad's cousin did not enter our discussion, but when he said to me on leaving, "That was an interesting conversation," I realized that for the first time I had stood apart and offered a critique with an unresolved answer.

I recalled that conversation more than a decade later when I was visiting my parents in New York; they had moved there when Dad joined an investment house. Dad had invited me to join them at a dinner party. The hostess was annoyed at having to serve an uninvited guest and squeezed me into a corner seat at the dinner table next to Dad. At Dad's left a woman turned and asked what he did for a living. Instead of answering her, he held out his left hand, licked the fingers of his right, and pretended to pick up something from his outstretched hand. When she asked what he was doing, he said, "counting money." His impish reply captured the difference between what he had done at Sears, which was producing goods for people at reasonable prices, and what he was doing on Wall Street, which was simply making money. He loved the one and was cynical about the other.

I remembered both experiences several decades later when I was attracted to the work of Thorstein Veblen (1922, 1942, [1904] 1978, [1899] 1979). He may be best known for his observations about conspicuous consumption in America at the turn of the twentieth century, but throughout his many books he distinguished between the "captains of industry," who made real things, and the "captains of finance," who made money from the work of the captains of industry. I melded his distinction between the realms of commerce and finance into the economic anthropology I developed.

***

My parents lived in Chicago through the worst of the Great Depression but at my birth moved to a suburb. If Dad's prospects at work had brightened when I was born, the world's had darkened. The European front of World War II began three months after my birth, and the United States entered the war after the bombing of Pearl Harbor in December 1941. In my early years, the country was on a war footing with food rationing, but after the war the US economy began expanding, and an optimistic air pervaded the suburb and public schools I attended. Most of my parents' friends were business people. This environment and especially my family emphasized academic achievement, but they did not prize scholarship itself. Chicago was a hub of commonsense behavior, and a career in medicine, law, or business seemed to be the appropriate destination.

Dad cherished thriftiness and value buying both personally and at work. To ease my mother when she was figuring what to have for dinner, Dad would say, "Yum, I love leftovers. Let's make do." Initially, I thought leftovers referred to a special food. Only later did I understand it meant searching in the refrigerator to put together bits and pieces from prior meals.

In French "making do" may be rendered as *bricolage*, a word brought to anthropological attention by Claude Lévi-Strauss (1962) in his comparative analysis of mythical thought, which uses and reuses a limited set of images like the leftover food in our refrigerator. New myths are arranged by making do with a stock of images as they pass between peoples and across generations. In contrast to Lévi-Strauss's attention to such figurative thinking, I use the expression "making do," which I often heard during fieldwork, to describe using tangible objects in a new way to get something done (although making do with material things also draws on figurative thinking).

Eventually I saw eating leftovers as Dad's pleasure in being thrifty. He soaked off stamps that had not been postmarked (I learned later that the practice is illegal). I watched him carefully preserve his clothes and not buy anything more than he would use. We never purchased the top-of-the line refrigerator or washing machine, because the lower cost ones had the same mechanism without the unnecessary appurtenances.

I absorbed the same lesson about thrift when Dad spoke about Sears products. We never used the word "cheap" for the company's goods, and if I did say "cheap," he corrected me. The proper term was "inexpensive," because cheap referred to a shoddily made object. For us, value meant quality goods sold at a fair price.

Years later, when I discovered the importance of "making economies" for the peasants in Panama and Colombia, I immediately understood they meant being thrifty and recorded the variety of practices to which the expression applied. Eventually, the idea of thrift became a theme in my understanding of the house as a form of economy that is quite different from a profit-seeking corporation.

Through precollege years I enjoyed math and social studies and subsequently entered Harvard never expecting to be an academic. I could not imagine spending years after graduation studying for a Ph.D. and could only picture myself as being stuffed with useless knowledge when I finished a higher degree. At the end of my freshman year, undecided about a major or "concentration," I attended a meeting in the Freshman Union where professors talked about their different fields. When it came to anthropology, an older man, who looked like a dried fish, took the floor. He was wearisome, and the field sounded boring. After the meeting, I walked across the street and just as I was in front of the undergraduate library, I said to myself, "I don't know what I want to do, but I know one thing, I will never be an anthropologist."

In the following years I became interested in social theory through courses taught by Talcott Parsons. He was developing a theory of social action, showing how actions are systematically connected and fit into a hierarchy based on different value orientations. He defined four pattern variables or values arranged in two binary oppositions, which were specific versus diffuse relationships, and pattern maintenance versus goal attainment. By crosscutting the two oppositions he generated a four-cell table in which each cell delineated a sector of society: religion, the polity, law, and the economy. Each cell contained another four-cell table, which contained another lower one. All fit neatly into the hierarchy that was governed by the four-part table composed of the crosscutting values. Parsons used the schema to distinguish the major constituents of a social system, which were culture, society, economy, and "behavioral organism," and each of these subjects had its avatar (Max Weber, Emile Durkheim, Adam Smith, and Charles Darwin).

I was not convinced but exposure to Parsons whetted my appetite for social theory, alerted me to the idea of unvoiced social values, and helped me place the anthropology I later learned and practiced. Parsons emphasized the significance of culture, or values and ideation, in relation to how people interact. When I eventually studied anthropology, I saw that his distinction pointed to the difference between US cultural anthropology with its emphasis on mentalities and British social anthropology that focused on social relationships. During my graduate fieldwork adopting a cultural focus helped me sort through the practices and interactions I was witnessing, although that perspective was not part of my British training.

College courses had other effects on the anthropology I later practiced. As a sophomore, I enrolled in the introductory course on economics. During the autumn, we learned about supply and demand curves and the effect of monopolies on pricing. As an example of the latter, the graduate student teaching assistant talked about the monopoly power of Sears Roebuck and how through buying power it squeezed its suppliers in order to undercut its competitors in refrigerators and washing machines.

Dad had been that Sears buyer for refrigerators and washing machines and first made his name by working with the manufacturers and helping them develop their products, such as Coldspot and Whirlpool.

I heard story after story about the way Sears worked with its suppliers and assisted them to reach consumers under their own brand names in order not to be overly reliant on Sears. Often, when the owners of these manufacturing firms came to Chicago, they stayed at our house, had dinner with us, talked with me, and shared my bathroom. They enjoyed great financial success with Sears.

In class I raised my hand and said, "I have met some of these suppliers. Sears encourages them to sell their products separately under their own brand name as well as to Sears. Many have done extraordinarily well financially."

"You're wrong," the teaching assistant responded, and reiterated that a single powerful buyer, according to the diagram he had drawn on the board, upset the standard picture of perfect markets and competitive pricing. He added, "You do not understand how the model works."

I understood the model as well as the difference between it and what I knew through experience. I left the course after one semester because the models and calculations in economics, though quite understandable with the math I knew, seemed removed from the way people actually behave in economic life. Eventually I returned to economics but to a wayward trail in the discipline.

My scholarly interests sharpened in my junior year when I attended a small seminar taught by the anthropologist, Cora Dubois. She told us stories from the field including the time that she sat on the edge of a canoe and urinated with local men watching in the bow and stern. I liked her open teaching and willingness to respond to students' critiques. As the semester progressed, I asked her about doing fieldwork in archaeology. She suggested that I see Evon Vogt who would be taking undergraduates to Mexico in the summer. I imagined a grand dig, went to meet Vogt and quickly learned the venture would be fieldwork with people. I knew little about this kind of study but was intrigued, and Vogt was enthusiastic and friendly. Ill-equipped though I was, he selected me with five others for the program and so began my introduction to field anthropology more by serendipity than by planning.

***

I read a few books about Mexico and started to learn Spanish in the late spring. When the summer began, I found myself in the town of San Cristobal in the southern Mexican state of Chiapas. Within days, Vogt deposited me in the little settlement of Chilil that was reached by Land Rover over a long and bumpy mud road.

Chilil, located about 8,000 feet above sea level, lies within the municipality of Huixtán, which corresponds roughly with a Mayan language group. I had learned that each Indigenous group wore a distinctive dress. As he drove me to the settlement, Vogt with his distinctive chuckle told me what to expect. His description was accurate. The men wore white shirts and shortened white pants that reached below the knees and were held up by a sash. The pants looked to me like a giant diaper. They had a broad flap that came from the back and was held in the front by the sash. The pants were never revealing. The women were a different story, which had brought the smile to Vogt's face, because he knew a young man would enjoy their garb.[1] Women wore a long dark full skirt, but their tops, under which they had nothing on, were slit on both sides and often flapped open. I never figured out how women stayed warm.

I was placed in an unfinished, very small two-room plaster dwelling. My cot just fit in one room, and I had a wooden table and chair squeezed into the other. Living directly next door was an Indigenous family. They had a stick and thatch house and spoke Tzeltal, their Mayan dialect. The man commanded some Spanish, which was slightly better than mine, but his spouse and young children did not.

The family fed me as we sat around their hearth on low stools that rocked on the uneven, earthen floor. The house was dark and lit only by the fire that was on the floor and surrounded by several stones on which the cooking vessels sat. The money I provided paid for the food that all of us ate. At night, the pair often seemed to fight in Tzeltal, which I supposed from their voices and her crying, although I knew not about what.

Three times a day I ate tortillas folded around potatoes and occasionally beans. I liked watching the tortillas being made and would arrive early to see the final stages of a long process. Kneeling on the ground, the woman broke off a lump of corn dough, added lime, and rolled the mixture on a smooth stone. Picking up a small piece of the dough, she patted it between her hands into a thin, circular shape, which she placed on the heated clay griddle. While preparing another tortilla, she would stop to flip the heating ones at the right moment. One after another a warm tortilla was filled with potatoes or beans. They were delicious. The following day I would have rewarmed tortillas with potatoes for breakfast and lunch.

I had learned about the Mexican food triad consisting of maize, beans, and squash. The three crops provide nutrients to each other in the soil and a balanced diet for humans. I was eating the tortilla part of the triplet but was served beans about three times a week and never saw squash. My neighbors did not raise enough maize even for themselves and were using the money I provided to supply most of the food for all of us. (In that summer of 1960, John Kennedy was running for the presidential nomination. After reading my field notes, Vogt often told the story that while Kennedy spoke about the poverty he saw in the coal mining areas of Appalachia where people ate only beans, I was eating potatoes.)

Lacking a store, the village had only a small clinic that was infrequently visited by a doctor or nurse. The population consisted of impoverished people who, lacking land elsewhere, had been moved to this relatively new village located on hilly, rocky, infertile land. During my stay, there were no collective meetings, rituals, or festivals, although they were held in other villages.

My task was to find out something about the way a "native" people lives and had done so traditionally, an assumption I did not question. I turned to "economy" not by knowledge or by theoretical or personal interest but from lack of seeing anything else to do. I watched men with hoes on their shoulders walk to their fields every day and followed them on occasion to observe part of the agricultural cycle that consisted of digging up and turning over the earth around the growing maize. I made notes about the hoeing but did not understand much about what I was seeing.

I had no tools for understanding any form of agriculture not to speak of economy. I knew the people were practicing a traditional way of farming but never completely learned why the villagers were located on such poor soil except that they had been brought together some years before from even poorer conditions. The Mexican government's Instituto Nacional Indigenista was helping them, but I saw little of this assistance other than the shelter that had been built for a visiting doctor or nurse. The other undergraduates were placed in established and organized villages as I later learned.

At night it was very cold. My unfinished house had open windows, a roof set above the plaster walls, and no heating. I tried to read by a kerosene lamp, but it shed little light. I wore my clothes in a sleeping bag and went to my neighbors for water that had been boiled but did not bathe in the village for lack of facility. As for defecation, which was not frequent, I would wander onto a nearby hill, look around, and drop my pants. I knew I had the right place because I had to watch my step as my hidden location was clearly used by many others. I felt my lack of a place to excrete symbolized my intellectual position, which was nowhere.

Over the summer, my Spanish improved a little, and my knowledge of the people an equally small amount. I was more a live-in tourist than an anthropologist. I knew only what I saw and felt distant from the people but enjoyed the simplicity of the food and clothing, and not being surrounded by unneeded goods. I had something of an intellectual life through books I was reading but had little idea about the life of the people among whom I was living. I could see how to hoe around maize, but how did it fit anything else? I was too naïve to ask or figure out how to ask.

From time to time, the undergraduate group would emerge from our sites to meet in the larger town, San Cristobal, and discuss our findings with the teaching assistant after Vogt left for Europe. We stayed at a humble tourist house, Na Bolom, run by an émigré couple. He was Danish, and she had a German accent and manner. He always dressed in a colorful costume with white shirt, red sash, and blue flowing bloomers, which was almost a mockery of the local dress. An older man, who claimed to be an anthropologist—he was really an old-style adventurer—told stories about landing in Chiapas by small airplane in the 1920s and exploring Mayan ruins. I would see him roaming about his room, rather drunk, pretending to work, and emitting loud farts. I could accept the latter but every time I stayed at their place I came down with the runs. When it happened, usually after a day of their food, I would walk some distance to the town pharmacist in the central plaza who would lead me behind his wooden counter while the front entrance remained open. I lowered my pants and bent over while peeping above the counter to see who was watching. He would inject me with a liquid that sometimes helped. I never saw him clean the needle before or after. This painful part of my experience was not helped back in the hamlet where a dog in a nearby house would emerge to bite me where the injections went. I was caught between my lower-than-Appalachia diet in the village and eating better in the town at the cost of the runs, injections, and having my behind become a dog's bone.

It was not an easy summer. Only later did I learn that a few years earlier Vogt had placed a graduate student in the hamlet. After a few days he found it so lonely that he left, and I do not know if he pursued anthropology. The other students in my group were far better situated in larger, more cohesive, and settled villages. Only midway through the summer did I learn that I was in a relatively new hamlet that was an agglomeration of transplanted people from other villages lacking cultivable land, many of whom did not know one another. After the summer I found out that Cora Dubois, who had recommended me, wrote that I was "tough-minded," which must have led Vogt to put me in the most difficult of the locales.

My mental image of the village and tiny shelter, of being cold and baffled about the life I saw, remained with me for years, and often comes to mind when I think about economic underdevelopment, although I hardly knew the phrase then. I was interested in grand social theory, but it provided few intellectual supports because at the time it divided societies into the "traditional" and the "modern," and all I could visualize was people with hoes over their shoulders walking to their fields and the way tortillas are made over a fire. The experience had a formative impact, however, for I could not make sense of the way the people lived, and this lack of understanding why other people do as they do still motivates my anthropology. I had lived in a village located at the margin of usable resources and concerns of the larger society, and I could not make sense of it.

Based on the summer's experience, I wrote a thesis on Highland Maya economies under Vogt's supervision. Even then I did not know what I wanted to do and had never taken a course in anthropology. Feeling uneducated, I was attracted to the idea of continuing my education in England and was awarded a Marshall Scholarship, which are two-year fellowships offered by the British government in appreciation for Marshall Aid after World War II.

## Note

1. I always recall Vogt ("Vogtie") for his kindness and his interest in my career after college. When remembering an experience that pleased him, Vogt chuckled with amusement and delight, and took pleasure in his students whom he treated as extended family.

CHAPTER 2

# The Two Cambridges

The scholarship began in September 1961. The group gathered in New York, sailed to England on the Queen Mary, and spent a few days in London for orientation meetings. The advice I thought most important was to open a bank account for deposit of the Marshall funds. Then I was on my way to Cambridge by train. I selected Cambridge because it offered a two-year undergraduate degree that turned into an MA after six years, if one preserved good behavior though I don't know if they checked on me after I finished the BA. I chose to read social anthropology because it was the closest offering to sociology I could find, and I selected King's College because it had the most anthropology dons or Fellows.

I took a taxi from the Cambridge station that after winding through narrow streets deposited me at King's. Entering through a wooden door, cut into a pair of very large wooden doors that served as gates, I went to the porter's lodge directly inside and found my luggage. With it in hand, I walked forward to the front lawn, which was the greenest grass I had ever seen and looked to my right where the college Chapel sat shimmering in the sun. Religious I am not but at that moment I knew I had come to the right place. I was free to experience British life, find new interests and friends, and let academic studies fit themselves to those happenings.

Within a day, I received a note from my supervisor to meet him at the porter's lodge. A tall, gangly and shaggy-looking man appeared. It was Edmund Leach. I knew he was well known, although I did not know for what, as I had not read any of his work or that of any British anthropologist. His jacket was askew, which it usually was, as if it did not fit him. His hands, moving and expressive when he talked, were enormous, and his arms seemed too long for his jacket. When he wore a tie, it was never straight. His hair might be combed in the early hours of the day, or when he straightened it before a meeting but was usually ruffled. He did not seem to notice how he looked. But there he was.

Not knowing what to do, he decided to walk me about the college, show me the buildings and library, and talk as we walked. I found straightaway that only dons were allowed to walk on the grass in the front and back courts of the college, and in the Fellows' garden. With Leach I could tread on it. For years I harbored the desire to walk on this sacred ground, which was a marker of intellectual superiority.

As we ambled, Edmund kept saying, "I don't know what I can teach you" after I uttered a few words about the sociology I had studied. He kept laughing or rather giggling as we walked, and I did not know what to make of it, except that he seemed ill at ease and possibly nervous. Our walk did not last long, and at the end he asked me to show up two days later at his office.

I arrived at the appointed time in my newly acquired black gown that had to be worn at supervisions (tutorials). Leach had on a gown but it was askew over his three-piece suit that also was awry. Scarcely had I sat down in an old, uncomfortable wooden chair across from him when an older man in a three-piece suit entered, pointed at a bookshelf, and said, "I want to borrow this book."

Leach stood up and replied, "You can't have that because you haven't returned the other one." The visitor grabbed the book, and he and Edmund began to pull on it and tussle. I sat there watching these grown men struggle and thought, "Now what have I gotten myself into?"

Eventually they stopped and I learned the entrant was Reo Fortune. We were not introduced. The first of my weekly supervisions had begun.

Reo had experienced a difficult marriage and divorce from Margaret Mead. They separated in New Guinea when she left him for Gregory Bateson who joined them in the field. Previously Fortune had written a mesmerizing book about the people on the South Pacific island of Dobu where lineages of yams—from tuber seeded, to harvest, to eating and back to seeding—were treated like lineages of humans as traced through women. A man tends and keeps separate the yams he inherited from his mother, and a woman tends and keeps separate the yams she inherited through her mother, although they cultivate their yams in the same garden plot.

By means of sorcery men try to steal the yams and the women of others because yams can walk about at night, and without yams a man loses his social position, can only fish for a living, and is despised.

Twenty-five years after encountering Fortune in Leach's office, I reanalyzed his study to show that economic practices on Dobu are a ritual. The Dobuan yam economy has nothing to do with supply, demand, and markets, or with central planning. The way yams are seeded, tended, held, distributed and consumed is a ritualistic way of addressing a tension in Dobuan life.

Principal connections on Dobu are traced through females. A woman is most closely related to her mother, sister, and children who belong to her matriline. A man is connected to his mother, sister, and sister's children in his matriline, plus his offspring. The residential group is the nuclear family that consists of the two parents and their children. As a result, a man is pulled toward his children with whom he lives but who belong to his spouse's matrilineage, and toward his sister and her children in the matrilineage of which he is a member, for they are his successors and inheritors. Dobuans manage this double pull by having the nuclear family stay together as a unit but shift its residence every year between the husband's and the wife's matrilineal villages. In one year, a man as mother's brother is united with his sister and his offspring along with his spouse. The next year, he and his children are united with their mother's brother who is their lineage elder. A matrilineage shares its males to father offspring in another lineage and to live with them every other year. It keeps its females to reproduce its descendants but lets them reside with an in-marrying male's matrilineage every other year. The core of the matrilineage, consisting of a mother and her children, is always together with the proviso of this residential sharing, and with the detriment that the in-marrying male is treated as a stranger when residing in the village of his spouse. Anthropologists before me had recognized and discussed this inherent friction on Dobu and in other matrilineal systems.

I saw something else in this intriguing lineage system. A generation after meeting Fortune, I was riveted by the Dobuan yam economy and began to see it as a ritual. The Dobuan economy based on yams does what a lineage cannot. Husband and wife, as they move back and forth between their natal villages, keep their lineage yams separate, and each line of yams is never distributed to people outside the lineage or mixed with yams from other lineages. In contrast, Dobuans, both females and males, must be exogamous or marry outside their matrilineage to procreate with the tensions and residential shifts this creates. Yam lines connected to a matrilineage are kept "endogamous" or separate from other yam stocks. They are intact strings of seed. The Dobuan economy based on yams achieves what matrilineages cannot, which is to bar outsiders from mixing with them. The yam economy, like a ritual, presents the way social life should be, just as our rituals exemplify proper behavior. But the Dobuan economy also turns our revered ideas upside down. Instead of providing the grounding, the material base, for social life, Dobuan economy is a ritual about the way life should be, enclosed and separate from others, or self-sufficient.

I encountered Reo many times after that meeting in Leach's office, sometimes in the street, when he was returning from a lecture in physics and would encourage me to study science rather than anthropology. Toward the end of my graduate career when I gave a talk to the department setting out my analysis of godparenthood, Reo boomed from the back, "Who do you think you are, God?" I could not think of a response, but the outburst seemed fitting given Reo, his way of seeing the world, my topic, and Cambridge seminars that were filled with critical comments and put-downs, although afterward the faculty and graduate students shared a beer or sherry.

***

The substance of my Cambridge education came through the weekly meetings or "supervisions" with Edmund, which were the best learning experiences I have had. I should have taken notes when he talked, but I was listening closely and too naïve to realize the opportunity. Always I had read a book or set of articles in anthropology for the week and was expected to write a brief essay about them and discuss the reading, which I would do for about ten to fifteen minutes. Edmund then commented not about what I said but about the broader issues raised by the reading. His words always seemed incisive, profound, and expansive. He would relate the book to his thinking and that of others, and do so with excitement. Often, he placed the tips of his fingers of his right hand in front of his mouth or on his lips as if pondering just before talking, and the size of his fingers and hand magnified the effect.

A few days later, I received handwritten notes on my paper or a concisely typewritten commentary that went to the heart of the subject. Sometimes Edmund provided a long explanation of a related and important topic in anthropology. Through these individual sessions I learned Leach anthropology, which was critical thinking followed by a creative response.

Through that first year, Edmund would tell me to read what I wanted. I had no background in anthropology and hardly knew where to turn, so I read theoretical works in anthropology. Eventually he suggested I should "concentrate on the drier aspect of the social anthropologist's kinship theory." So, I read traditional studies about lineages and kinship, which are especially dry, and supplemented them with doses of A. R. Radcliffe-Brown (an earlier professor of anthropology at Oxford who helped inspire many kinship studies) but did not find the subject or that author interesting. When I remarked to Edmund that Radcliffe-Brown seemed rather like Talcott Parsons, he sniffed, but I think I was correct because both were "structural functionalists" who were tantalized by the idea that society is a naturalistic or mechanistic system that achieves equilibrium and remains static. Edmund often engaged in battles over this older, equilibrium idea, which he seemingly rejected, and I understood his sniff as a critique of both theorists, although it could have been my equation of the limpid Radcliffe-Brown with the abstruse Parsons that he was dismissing. Eventually, when Edmund explained that learning the technical analysis of kinship systems is like learning a language that once acquired becomes easy to use, I became an inconstant addict of those studies with their static diagrams of patrilineages, matrilineages and much more. They were fascinating although later it emerged that they were often the anthropologist's and not the people's construction.

Edmund had a way of talking in supervisions and lectures that made listeners feel he was telling them something new, something uncovered. Often, he started a lecture, essay or supervision by debunking a prior theory. Then he stated his contrary idea. Like the charismatic teacher that he was, Leach effectively said, "It is stated, but I say onto you . . ." He took the listener through a rite of passage that ended with his position. Edmund was a performer and very difficult to imitate, although many of us tried. His ideas about ritual, kinship, and structuralism became part of my bones that took years to rinse out.

Leach's intimations in supervisions and lectures, conveyed by his hands and elliptical phrases, that he was discovering something no one had thought about before have stayed with me, for they made me realize: "Why do anthropology unless it harbors discoveries?" Always stimulating, Leach's supervisions became special moments when he seemed inspired and inspired me. Afterward, I felt that nothing could be more important than anthropology, and even if I did not take notes, which would have diverted my attention, I learned more anthropology through these private times with him than by reading him or attending his lectures. Years later I could still hear his voice and picture his movements on a topic.

The supervisions were held late in the afternoon, so a glass or two of sherry accompanied the meeting. I do not know if the alcohol slowed or heightened my responses and concentration, but I emerged from the sessions, often carrying a book on loan from Edmund, convinced that anthropology held the key to understanding the human world. Usually, night had fallen and Cambridge was damp, but I did not notice. Even if it took me some time deciding to become an anthropologist, I would never have become one without those supervisions. Many years later, when I read John Maynard Keynes's tribute to Alfred Marshall, his teacher at Cambridge, I knew exactly what he was talking about.

> The pupil would come away with an extra-ordinary feeling that he was embarked on the most interesting and important voyage in the world. He would walk back along the Madingley Road, labouring under more books, which had been taken from the shelves for him as the interview went on, than he could well carry, convinced that here was a subject worthy of his life's study . . . The subject itself had seemed to grow under the hands of master and pupil, as they had talked. There were endless possibilities, not out of reach. (Keynes: 1924: 366)

About once a month after supervision, Leach invited me to join his wife Celia and him for dinner, and he would drive me to their house on Storeys Way. Celia was a marvelous cook and served dishes I did not know, such as pheasant with buckshot on the inside. She cooked on a huge Aga stove that was heated by a wood fire, which Leach would feed as the cooking progressed. On occasion we went to a pub or elsewhere for dinner.

***

When spring arrived at the end of my first year, I began to think about the coming summer. Dad was in Washington, and since I was interested in government policy and its relation to people, I asked him about finding a relevant position for the summer. He came up with several possibilities, some in Washington and one in Massachusetts working for Ted Kennedy who was starting a run for his brother's now open Senate seat that would be contested in the autumn. I chose Massachusetts to work in his campaign. Kennedy's opponent was the Republican, George Cabot Lodge, the son of the previous senator, Henry Cabot Lodge, whom John Kennedy had bested in their Senate race before becoming president. Several years later, Ted Kennedy's opponent and my interest in government policy converged and had a significant consequence for my anthropological career.

When I arrived in Massachusetts, I was put on the top floor of a small building in downtown Boston that served as the campaign's headquarters. Telephone calls and visits for help were directed to me. The callers and visitors usually wanted assistance finding a job or a welfare program. I made notes for others in the campaign who might be able to find a proper contact in social services or a job agency. I also met with innumerable people that I could not help and usually felt emotionally exhausted at the end of the day.

After several weeks, I was moved to the central floor of campaign headquarters where I assisted the speechwriters. They were friends and acquaintances of Kennedy from their years together at Harvard law school. I hung out with them or with the campaign manager after hours or on the weekend. I was paid every two weeks in cash without presenting my social security number or signing a contract.

Occasionally we accompanied Kennedy when he campaigned in Boston, and I saw his charisma and facility relating to people. He rode in the back of a convertible, standing up, waving, and smiling at the crowds on both sides of the road. He was informal looking without a tie but wore expensive shirts unbuttoned at the collar. Sometimes we passed the three buses of the Lodge campaign, which was the totality of his much less funded campaign, as Lodge later told me.

Some weekends we went to Hyannis Port on the Cape where the Kennedy Compound was located. We played softball and football (a favorite of the Kennedys) on their big lawn and Kennedy joined us. On occasion we went out on one of the Kennedy yachts for a party. Sometimes Ted (or "The Candidate" as he was known to campaign workers) climbed aboard from another yacht to join us and have a drink. He was charming.

When I was asked to revise some of Kennedy's drafts for speeches, I was less impressed. Handed a sequence of his versions for a speech about the Guinea leader, Sekou Toure, who disliked President Eisenhower and admired President Kennedy, I saw the same laudatory phrases were switched about and used repeatedly with little substance about Guinea or Sekou Toure's accomplishments. Ted's strength was connecting with people.

At the compound, we would occasionally see President Kennedy on a yacht or at a distance. One time I was driving a group of us on a single lane road when we came face-to-face with JFK driving his convertible. He and I stopped our cars, and everyone jumped out to shake his hand. I sat as I felt it mattered little whether or not I shook his hand, but perhaps that was youthful arrogance. Another time we toured each of the family houses. Shortly before, relations with Cuba had soured, and the United States had placed an embargo on trade with the island. When we were going through the president's house and reached the dining room, I noticed a large humidor on the sideboard. I peeked, as I did with other items in the house, and saw a large collection of Cuban cigars, which were contraband. I wondered how they got there and thought about the privileges of power and adhering to the law. Forty years later, when I made several anthropological trips to Cuba, I found Kennedy's brand of cigar, which was also Fidel Castro's favorite, the Cohiba. Given the Hyannis Port experience, I smuggled home a vast quantity in my shoes and enjoyed the smoothness, the smell, and the perfect leaf wrapping of the best cigar in the world.

I was staying on a couch in my cousin's apartment, when the campaign manager offered me the president's apartment on Beacon Hill in Boston, which was unoccupied. I moved there. This small, unadorned place, except for the pictures of Kennedys that covered the walls, had been his legal residence while a Massachusetts Senator. I enjoyed living in the president's apartment and being reminded every night of the family's wealth and power but dared not invite visitors. I used the bedroom and toilet but not the small kitchen.

When the summer came to an end, Ted asked if I would stay through the campaign with the possibility of going to Washington should he win in November, but I decided to return to Cambridge for the second year to finish my degree. By then I knew I did not want a career in politics or government administration. It seemed less intellectual than I desired, not fully in touch with material life, and unpredictable.

***

Only in my second year at King's, after the rugby season ended, did I study anthropology and learn what it was about. I found Cambridge life so stimulating that until the final two terms of the second year, I was attending lectures on architecture, reading widely from novels to the memoirs of George Kennan, going to films with friends, and talking endlessly with others at dinner and afterward besides playing college rugby and tennis on the college's grass courts.

Despite this involvement in an idyllic college life, I always felt a bit of a visiting anthropologist because some of the rituals were strange. Dinner in college hall began with the clanging of a gong once the undergraduates had gathered in their gowns and were standing at their tables, followed by the senior members in their gowns who marched to their high table that was set on a platform at one end of the dining hall. A prayer in Latin was uttered, but never having studied Latin, I didn't understand a word. Students sat on wooden benches at tables made of rough wood. Male waiters dressed in black trousers, white shirts and black ties brought a tasteless soup followed by dishes of over-cooked vegetables (often brussels sprouts), boiled potatoes, and a dish of boiled meat, which was usually mutton but sometimes beef, though I could not always tell the difference. I observed from a distance this combination of mock splendor, coarse wooden furniture, tasteless food, and service by well-dressed older men to hungry young men wearing black gowns. Dinner was a ritual modeled after upper class manners but without much savor.

Lunch was also served but it was informal, and the Fellows sat with us. One time late in my first year, I found myself sitting across from Patrick Wilkinson who (though I did not know) had just been elected vice provost of the college. I also did not know that he assigned rooms for undergraduates. We must have had a good conversation, because in my second year I found myself in a large two-room suite just below John Maynard Keynes's old suite in Webb's court. It was the prime undergraduate chamber.

My bedroom had a washbasin, but the toilets were two flights below in the cold basement. The wooden seats were freezing and not conducive to extended reading or sitting. I never fully mastered flushing these toilets by pulling the chain on the tank that was on the wall above. Sometimes I stood on a cold night waiting for the tank to refill and giving it another try, but I was consoled that a Kingsman, Thomas Crapper, invented the flush toilet, and toilets seemed to be his legacy to the college. My bedroom basin saved many visits to the cellar.

E. M. Forster, who was short and frail by 1962, lived in college and had meals served to him in his rooms by the porters. One night a friend arranged for a few of us to meet this literary giant. We gathered in a large room in the Gibbs building. Five of us sat in front of Forster as he read from his best-known book, *A Passage to India*. He used a paperback version and read slowly. Soon, he fell asleep in midsentence, and we sat there, waiting and unsure what to do.

When he woke up, he continued and then asked for questions. One bright undergraduate asked him the obvious one, "What really happened in the Marabar Caves?" which is the enigmatic moment on which the story hinges. Forster must have been asked this question many times, and he answered, "I don't know," which I thought was appropriate given the novel and a very undergraduate question.

A. C. Pigou, who had been an undergraduate at King's and later succeeded Marshall as the professor of economics, lived in college. Pigou, who died before I arrived, was a friend of Keynes, although Keynes attacked him in his own writings. As he grew older, Pigou increasingly stayed in his rooms at King's and rarely bought clothes to the point that his jackets were threadbare. His clothing condition came to a head when the Italian prime minister visited Cambridge and wanted to meet the famous economist. The college had to find a proper jacket for Pigou so that neither he nor the college would be embarrassed at his condition. An expert on numbers and taxes as well as other calculations, Pigou had calculated the probability of his life span and had stopped buying clothes because he gauged that he would die before his current ones wore out. I am enamored of the story for the sense of thrift and calculation lived by an economist, the fact that economists sometimes get it wrong, and especially because Pigou's practices fit my love of thrift.[1]

I felt surrounded by marvelous minds, but some college rituals I viewed with incredulity. The provost of King's was Noel Annan, later Baron Annan after he left King's. In the autumn of my first year, he led those who had just entered the College on a brief tour of King's. As we walked about King's, Annan spoke briefly about the history of the Chapel, the different buildings, the library, and particularly about John Maynard Keynes whose great book (*The General Theory of Employment, Interest and Money*) he happened to have in hand, which he lofted and waved in the air. We then descended to a basement room containing the college's stock of wine, which was served to the Fellows at High Table, and to a locked room that held the college silver. It was a vast collection of wine goblets, serving plates, jugs, tongs, tea sets, candle sticks, and beer mugs, accumulated by gifts over hundreds of years. Many of the objects were brought out for the Fellows to use at college feasts (as the elaborate dinners were called). As we gazed on the shiny collection, the provost said, "Boys, before you die, remember the college silver in your will." I was astounded by the historical collection but even more because the college did so little to solicit money for its endowment. I stood there thinking I would have sold the silver and invested the money.

This sense of preeminence may have been due to the endowment of the College that had increased immeasurably half a century earlier when Keynes as bursar managed the college funds and separately made a fortune for himself. He reallocated the College's assets from agricultural land, some of which had come as grants from the Crown, to diverse equities and anticipated by many years the asset allocation models of Wall Street that began to be formulated only in the 1970s. By the time of Keynes's death in 1946, King's was one of the richest colleges in Cambridge, and possibly the wealthiest per capita.

Today I might not be so judgmental about the College's stock of silver objects, its dead assets. In my approach to economy, I emphasize the significance of accumulating and holding a legacy or base that maintains a community of people. As a stock of things that are never sold, and that link the past with the present, the base provides a tangible identity for an economy built on social relationships. The heirlooms of King's signify the College's enduring status, and their occasional appearance at festive occasions is a ritual of solidarity with the past and a portend of the future. The walls of the College are dotted with portraits of past Fellows, and stories about them are passed across generations. Partly with these experiences in mind, as well as the priceless Chapel and choir, I turned to the concept of a legacy or base during fieldwork in Colombia as I considered the way a people conceive and construct their economy.

In the autumn of 1962, I continued to play rugby but with less interest and at the turn of the year finally applied myself to anthropology. Toward the end of the academic year, I sat the two-year exams. After the exams, Meyer Fortes asked if I was interested in pursuing a PhD and said he had access to funds for a graduate student to work in Thailand. I spoke to Edmund who scoffed, "That's CIA money." I was not ready to commit to a career in anthropology, anyway. Earlier in the year, I had applied to the Harvard Business School contemplating the possibility of entering the business world and Wall Street as I remained interested in the way economy really works.

***

Returning to Cambridge (Massachusetts) in the autumn of 1963, I resumed seeing Roxane whom I had met at the very end of my senior year in college, but we lost contact when I went to England. By this time, she had completed a master's degree in educational psychology at Harvard, and when I returned, she was a graduate student in developmental psychology at the Graduate School of Arts and Sciences. We became constant companions and married in 1965 when I finished business school two years later.

If I had high expectations for learning about practical economics at the Business School, they were dashed. I wanted to know about everyday economy, commerce and manufacturing, about consumers and what people need, and about organizations. My fellow students were interested in making money. They dressed as young business people, so I acquired a low-cost suit and white shirt to look like the others but soon shifted to different clothing.

We were taught that good administrative practices could be switched from one business to another regardless of what was being produced. The ideology fitted the times, for "conglomerates" or corporations embracing a variety of unrelated holdings through money management had become popular and honored. Some of these leaders were brought to the school to speak about their careers, but I never fathomed what advantage they provided to consumers or the larger society, and more than a few seemed to have stripped their acquired businesses of jobs and capital.

The largest department at the school was called human behavior in organizations, which I thought would be appealing, but the sociology theories it used presumed that human collectivities are equilibrating systems, an approach that anthropologists had jettisoned. A course or two focused on the relation of personality and organization, which I assumed would be attractive, but its psychoanalytic, post-Freudian perspective explained little about what happens inside a business.

I was troubled by the lack of morality that coursed through the school. If the students were interested in making money, the professors proclaimed that business was about "more" than making money but inevitably deployed a bottom-line metric on the argument that good management of people and organizations leads to profits. I never learned about the satisfaction of working with others or what more than making money meant, nor did they speak to a moral perspective that might influence the conduct of a business.

In a course on international business, the professor presented an example involving a US businessman conveying goods for sale in Mexico. At the border, a Mexican customs agent stopped him. As their encounter unfolded, the customs agent subtly asked for a bribe. Should the businessman pay, we were asked?

One student said, "He should bargain."

Others argued, "He should pay and get on with it."

One person suggested, "He should go to another point of entry."

No one suggested that he turn around.

After further discussion, the professor concluded that although paying a bribe was not a proper or legal way to conduct business in the United States, it was a custom in Mexico and the seller should conform. Perhaps the professor thought he was being anthropological. I was uncomfortable with his solution not because he would have viewed my answer—that bribing was not accepted in Mexican law, that paying for entry would promote the practice, and that professors usually do not provide "answers" to open-ended cases—as wrong, but because his answer legitimated the businessman's interest in the bottom line.

In a course on finance, I saw that corporations are made up of credits and debits, which I related to the anthropological notion of roles as consisting of rights and duties. I asked myself, "Is there a relation between corporate entities with assets and liabilities, and the reciprocal obligations of rights and duties that make up positions in society, as anthropologists then conceived it? Had anthropologists adopted a corporate view of society, or was it the reverse?"

Then I transposed the question. "How does the anthropological idea of reciprocity—or the uncalculated give-and-take between people in material life—fit a corporate perspective? What is the role in market economy of the unfigured back-and-forth of things and help that make social relationships in many societies?" The notion of reciprocity, which went back to Bronislaw Malinowski's study in the Trobriand Islands ([1922] 1961) and was developed by Marcel Mauss ([1925] 2016), had become a mainstay in economic anthropology. Where did it fit in the business world, or was there a profound difference between the economies that anthropologists study and market economies?

The professors at the Business School did not recognize a clash between ramping up the bottom line through impersonal market transactions and maintaining connections to others through the nonmonetary exchange of goods and services even in market societies. This tension in material life, which confronted me during my business education, later became a theme in my comparative view of economy.

Business training, however, had a useful impact on my later fieldwork. It gave me confidence to pursue a tangential or orthogonal (sinistral might be a better word, that is not right but left) economic anthropology that fits neither the expectations of economics proper nor of anthropology. Following business practices, I have never feared to make estimates in the field if precise calculations are lacking.

Students in the second year were required to provide a thesis based on research in the preceding summer. One professor suggested that I undertake an anthropological-like study of Arthur D. Little (ADL), which was a premier consulting firm located in the area. The vice president of the firm agreed to a study of their meetings with prospective clients provided that I never publish the results.

I spent the summer at ADL and attended many prospective client meetings, listening and taking notes. In some cases, the firm flew me with a team of consultants to other cities. I considered the research to be anthropology at home, although I did not ask questions in the meetings. I also learned about my taste for mid- to upper-level positions in business.

One morning I flew to Cleveland with a consultant to meet the assistant to the vice president of a large paint company. I expected a crisp discussion. What was the corporation's problem? How revealing would the executive be? I wanted some insights into the way a business operated and how a consultant connected to a potential client.

The executive's small office had one window that faced redbrick, older buildings. Narrow and rather tall, dressed in a white shirt with a thin tie held tight around his neck, he sat with his back to the window. The day was hot, the window was open, and the three of us were covered in perspiration. The executive talked and responded to questions but could not specify the problem the ADL man came to hear or reach a decision about using a consultant.

"Our sales are falling in some areas to a competitor."

"Why?"

"I am not certain."

"Have you asked people in your stores? Is it the price of your paint, its quality, or something else?"

"I don't know."

"How can Arthur D. Little help?"

"I don't know."

I continued taking my anthropological notes but was increasingly bewildered by the meeting. Sitting in front of the manager, my eyes began to wander out the window and over other buildings that partially reflected the hot sun. Finally, as the discussion dragged on, the three of us went up several floors to the office of the vice president. Dark and cool with an air conditioner, his office overlooked Lake Erie. In ten minutes, he asked about the problem and said, "We do not need a consultant." As we rode to the airport, I thought about the expense for both sides, the tiresome afternoon, and the complex interplay of personality, power, and rational decision-making in corporations.

A week later, after attending other meetings at ADL's headquarters, during which one consultant fell asleep after drinking wine at lunch and during another when two brothers complained that their unpatented invention for packaging cheese had been stolen by a larger corporation, I flew with a consultant to a New Jersey port where a firm that warehoused whiskey from abroad was experiencing problems with loss of its product. After an hour's discussion, it came to light that the longshoreman's union was stealing bottles from every shipment and slowing the work, which raised costs. The ADL man said to the manager, "There is nothing I can do." On the airplane home he told me, "I will not touch Mafia issues."

I did not find the consulting problems intellectually interesting, was not impressed with many of the organizations and people that I encountered, and did not want to be a consultant suggesting solutions to other people's problems yet left with no control over their implementation. I longed for a more theoretical approach and wanted to work on intellectual problems rather than practice an applied profession.

The summer's research provided material for a study, which I wrote in the autumn of my second year. I described the way meetings with prospective clients were like a rite of passage. The ADL people first introduced themselves and then listened to the prospective client's problem while guiding him into the possibility of change by their questions, hints, and persuasions. During this back-and-forth middle phase prospective clients might hear more about the larger issues involved, other information that might be needed, and the possibilities of resolution. This middle moment could be unsettling as the consultants gathered more information while the prospective client could be defensive about his or her lack of knowledge. Finally, a verbal proposal was offered and later a contract was agreed, revised, or rejected, and the three-phase rite of passage was complete.

The anthropological framework of a rite of passage, with its examples drawn from my observations, offered ADL an understanding of the process in which they were engaged, helped illuminate the successful and failed meetings with prospective clients, and provided suggestions for moving through the middle, in-between state. I showed that a business connection was both a rational bargain that involved the exchange of knowledge for money, and a ritual depending on persuasion and the evocation of trust.

## Note

1. I have often written about the House Economy that lies at the other end of the scale from the Market. It has several characteristics of which an important one is thrift. Pigou was practicing house economy thrift, albeit with an economist's eye. Thrift, as the propensity to hold or keep, is precisely what Keynes sought to combat in his famous 1936 book *General Theory of Employment, Interest and Money* ([1936] 2017), which was a macro theory of economy that showed how to break depressions through government spending when consumers do not and cannot spend. With tongue in cheek, I wonder if this difference about the place of thrift had to do with the gulf between Pigou and Keynes, who attacked his supporter numerous times in his book.

CHAPTER 3

# Panama and an Interlude

By the autumn of 1964 in my second year at the Harvard Business School, I decided to return to Cambridge for a PhD in anthropology. Then I met George Cabot Lodge, who was teaching a course on international business. George had joined the Business School after losing to Ted Kennedy in the contest for Massachusetts's senator when I worked for Ted two years before. George was the son of Henry Cabot Lodge, Jr., who had lost his senator's seat to John Kennedy in 1952. In 1963, however, President Kennedy appointed Henry Cabot Lodge, Jr. as the United States Ambassador to South Vietnam, where the war was raging.

The international perspective of the United States was changing. Enthused by the success of the Marshall Aid Plan after World War II that helped rehabilitate the UK and Europe, the Kennedy administration began fostering economic development in other parts of the world. Uniting and expanding several existing programs, the White House created the Agency for International Development (AID) under the umbrella of the US State Department. Throughout the 1960s AID focused on providing technical assistance and capital support to other nations.

Even before this time, dating back at least to Adam Smith, economists had been formulating models of economic growth. Now, stimulated by the experience of the Great Depression with its slow recovery, and by the growing "threat" of communism, economists increasingly attended to growth in less "dynamic" nations. One of the most prominent and popular writings of the era was a brief book by Walt Whitman Rostow that was published in 1960. *The Stages of Economic Growth: A Non-Communist Manifesto* was rather simple in conception and easy to read. Many of us had read or heard of it.

With the Vietnam War in mind, George Lodge was interested in ways to promote development in rural areas.[1] He had become acquainted with liberal Bishop Marcos McGrath in Panama who was starting a series of local cooperatives in the interior of the country. George wanted the Business School to be involved with this effort and suggested I might wish to be included. I was reminded of the dire situation I had seen in Mexico and the one development course I had taken at the Business School that had mostly to do with raising the GNP in other countries and little to do with impoverishment. The idea of studying and participating in local development work while undertaking a PhD combined my interests and attracted me.

With financial support from the Business School, I went to Panama in the summer of 1965 to look for fieldwork sites and become acquainted with the cooperative movement. I selected a small village that was in the territory of the budding cooperative program. The villagers had also recently begun raising sugarcane for cash sale as a supplement to their traditional crops of rice, maize, and tubers for home consumption. Studying a shifting combination of domestic provisioning and cash sale in the context of development seemed new and fit my interests.

On returning to Cambridge, Massachusetts, in the late summer, George and I worked out a project, took it to Washington, and presented it to the State Department and the Agency for International Development (AID), which was under the umbrella of the State Department. After several meetings in Washington, we took it for final approval to Rostow, who was now chairman of the State Department's Policy Planning Council and a strong supporter of the Vietnam War. After meeting in his office where I said nothing, for George already knew Rostow from his time in Washington and had read drafts of his book, we received his approval for a contract by which I would work for the Harvard Business School, which would receive funding for the project from AID.

By now I was a bit dizzy in this political situation with its overt, subtle, and contrary interests. George Lodge and I never discussed the Vietnam War that was influencing him through his father, the ambassador there, nor did the topic arise when we met Rostow. Lodge's interest in promoting rural development might have been double-sided. On one side, it represented reaching out to people in Panama who were living in conditions not unlike those of Vietnam as a preventative to the possibility of a rural uprising. On the other, our project was the opposite of waging war with rural folk and was inspired by the desire to do something to improve their welfare. From a different perspective, the promotion of cooperatives in rural Panama could be seen as an initial step moving them toward capitalism or was it a nudge toward socialism? I did not know what Rostow thought the outcome would be in light of his theory of modernization, and we had not framed it to fit his model.

I thought it curious that Rostow was a modernization theorist and anti-communist, but his socialist parents had named him after Walt Whitman, the American poet of the common people, while his two brothers were named after Ralph Waldo Emerson, the American transcendentalist, and after Eugene Debs, the famous turn-of-the-century American labor leader who ran for president as the candidate of the Socialist Party. I was caught in a mix of ideologies and intentions.

As for Bishop McGrath, I learned during the summer that his interests overlapped and differed from ours.[2] The bishop, who was tall, square-jawed, and sparing in lifestyle, was educated at Notre Dame. He always wore a black collar with white shirt and black coat. The bishop never looked hot or uncomfortable even when I was perspiring in the heat and humidity. His demeanor matched his physical presence. Speaking in an even voice, he never seemed bothered or flustered. Even when he told me a tale or two about a mischievous politician, his voice lacked emotion as if he were a reporter observing the scene. Always on the move, though not physically restless, he was never long seated for a conversation. Friendly, if at a distance, he was inwardly and outwardly committed to his calling and diligent in meeting his clerical obligations.

McGrath had been appointed Bishop of Veraguas Province in 1964 and five years later was named Archbishop of Panama. Liberation Theology was developing and expanding in Latin America during the 1950s and 1960s. This strand in Catholic thought, which was partly influenced by Marxist ideas, linked concern for the poor with political freedom. Liberation theology often used the concept of a "base community" that would reach peasants through the church and help them become more self-reliant. I never heard Bishop McGrath speak about liberation theology or base communities—he seemed too conventional for that—but clearly these themes were influencing his interest in promoting village cooperatives that would enable the people to have a better life and participate in the church. He once told me, however, that his purpose in promoting the cooperative movement was to enable the peasants to have funds that could help support the church in Panama.

At least my tasks were clear. I would study the small cooperative movement promoted by Bishop McGrath in the Panamanian countryside and explore its potential for helping the people. I would also produce some business cases for teaching in a new Central American business school that Harvard was supporting and promoting in Guatemala. The two projects, directed to the poor and to the elite, broadly fitted Rostow's interests, although he did not inspire them. Lastly, I would carry out fieldwork for my PhD at Cambridge while under contract with a US government agency. For a neophyte, it was a heady arrangement facilitated by Lodge's connections. In retrospect, I am amazed at the trust shown in me, even if the amount to be spent was small. I knew nothing about economic development, did not know how cooperatives worked, had never written a business case for teaching, was uncertain about my language abilities, and had never been a real field worker.

***

Roxane and I married in September 1965 after I returned from Panama. She was now in her second year as a graduate student in Developmental Psychology at Harvard, taking classes for a PhD but decided to begin her doctoral research ahead of schedule and focus on children's language learning in Panama, which fit her training and interests. We spent the autumn in Cambridge, England, so I could have a term there before beginning the field research.

By January 1966, we were in the small village of Los Boquerones, which is situated about 150 miles west of Panama City. Panama stretches from east to west. The Canal cuts through the country from northwest to southeast with Panama City at its northern end.

The nation is divided into ten provinces and three indigenous regions. Los Boquerones is located in the large central province, Veraguas, which is also known as "the interior" to city inhabitants. I sometimes met people in Panama City who claimed they had never been to the interior or had only passed through on their way to the city of David at the far end of the nation near the border with Costa Rica. The cement two-lane highway from Panama City into Veraguas had been completed only seven years before our arrival and the westward extension to David was still unfinished.

Veraguas province and its neighboring areas were never heavily populated (except perhaps before Columbus) and certainly not by wealthy people. Since independence from Spain, city dwellers had possessed the land and used some of it for extensive grazing. They allowed the local peasants or campesinos (country folk) to live on it and till portions in return for a few days of labor on their pastures.

The soil, lateritic and red looking once it was cleared of forest, was not very fertile. By our time, much of the original rain forest had been cleared in many of the lowland areas and was succeeded by scrub. Hot throughout the year, the area saw heavy rains in winter and blazing sun in the summer. Roxane calmly survived, but I was always sweaty and sapped. A clean shirt lasted a day, and my clothes smelled of mildew after washing. The few books I brought and took home smelled of mildew for years.

Our house was constructed of cinder blocks with a corrugated metal roof. A half wall divided its single room into a front area and a back kitchen that consisted of a tabletop two-burner propane stove and a small kerosene refrigerator that refused to stay lit or cold. One day a neighbor heard me swearing at it in my full range of English curses. She broke out laughing because she knew those English words but not others.

We slept under a mosquito net given the bugs, bats, scorpions, and other nightly callers. I shook out my shoes every morning in case scorpions had crawled into them. None ever sought refuge, but we cleared scorpions when using the one-hole privy in back of the house. We paid neighbor girls to haul water from a pump for drinking and cooking, and paid a widow to wash our clothes at a stream. Our nightly meal was most often spaghetti or rice, which we purchased sometimes from neighbors. It was occasionally garnished with canned tuna that we bought and brought from Panama City. When neighbors' chickens were obliging, we had eggs, and we bought tiny packets of ground coffee and buns at a small village store. The fare was slightly more varied than what I had eaten in Mexico. The campesinos usually ate their homegrown rice at every meal supplemented by the beans and maize they were able to raise.

At night, we lit a kerosene lamp, which attracted moths, made notes, and read or played games by the flickering flame. Sometimes we caught a shortwave radio band from the armed forces and heard about Vietnam. As we intermittently followed the huge three-month military operation, "Junction City," which was designed to destroy the "headquarters" of the Viet Cong, we doubted it would succeed, considering the general similarity of conditions where we were living and those of Vietnam. (For more than fifty years, the Darien jungle of Panama had been used by the US army to train troops in jungle warfare, a training center that was expanded during the Vietnam War.) I seldom forgot that the United States government and people supporting that expensive war also paid for my small research in Panama, which was a quest for a peaceful way to help rural people.

***

The funds I received from AID through the Business School supported almost two years of field research and obligated me to work in interwoven directions, anthropology and development. Both were based on my fieldwork and illuminated each other, as I found, but their purposes diverged and brought me into contact with different people.

Cambridge keeps a light hand once a student begins fieldwork, while my connections to the Business School and AID were robust. George Lodge and I frequently exchanged letters, and he came to Panama several times. He was a liberal Republican, who would be out of place in present times, had served in the Eisenhower administration, and met at times with Nixon when he was vice president under Eisenhower.

George, who was in his mid-thirties, had a cheerful and friendly disposition. Always informal and equalitarian with me, he gave me considerable freedom to define my tasks. George's face was hardly lined. He often smiled, and I never saw him act perturbed or concerned. Over time, as George and I talked, I learned that both his father and great grandfather had been senators from Massachusetts. As a youngster, he was driven to a private school in his father's limousine, but George would stop it a block away, so he could walk and not be seen alighting from the car. At the age of thirty-one, he had been appointed Assistant Secretary of Labor in the prior Eisenhower administration and subsequently was the US delegate to the International Labor Organization.

George learned to write professionally, he said, in college and as a reporter for the *Boston Herald*, and he told me stories about interviewing people immediately after a spouse or child had died. He never knew what to say, being torn between his reporting task and empathy. George also related his impressions of Nixon. For him, Nixon was different in public and private, where he was impressive and knowledgeable. Nixon, he said, was thoughtful, accomplished in foreign affairs, and sympathetic to the labor perspective, but George rarely criticized anyone.

We met in Cambridge, Boston, Panama City, and our Panama village. Of these places, George relished the latter, because he could see local life firsthand. One time, Roxane and I invited Lodge and Bishop McGrath to eat with us. We obtained four small pieces of meat with some difficulty and were ready to cook them when a dog barged into our dwelling, grabbed one of the pieces and ran off to eat it. I chased the thief into the forest, retrieved the meat, and dusted off the dirt and the dog's saliva. We cooked and served it with the other three pieces, not mentioning that one had been marinated in a dog's mouth. Having kept an eye on which it was, we served it to the bishop who we thought would have the best protection against perils.

In light of our collaboration, I found it ironic that only a few years earlier I had worked for Ted Kennedy in the senate race against George who lost to him, but Lodge gave it no mind. His father also had run for vice president (with Nixon) against John Kennedy in 1960, which added to the quirk of our work together, because directly before we met, Dad had served two years in the Kennedy administration.

I was expected to report periodically to the AID office in Panama City. At the time, the United States was providing more development money per capita to Panama than to any other country undoubtedly because of the strategic importance of the Canal, and because the Canal Zone was home to the largest US naval base for the Pacific. The agency's offices were located on the upper floors of a tall building in Panama City. At the top of the building a large sign read, *Cemento Panama*. James Bond films were popular then, and I always sardonically thought of the sign as cover for the top floor inhabitants who might be CIA.

The AID people were a varied group. Some were numbers people who showed me spreadsheets of the Panama economy with the lament that if only the Panamanians would follow their recommendations the economy would develop. Several times I invited them to visit us in the distant countryside to see conditions firsthand. No one accepted my offer, and in response they said that market centers should be built throughout the countryside to induce the people to produce their crops for sale. They kept to their air-conditioned offices.

Given our humble and humid living conditions, I was slightly envious of their air-conditioned life in apartments and offices with pleasant views. When I learned that AID employees in Panama City received a hardship allowance in addition to their salaries and as I was an employee of AID through the Business School, I once asked the local administrator, "Shouldn't I receive a hardship allowance given where we live and our living conditions?" I thought it was a logical request.

He responded, "Your village does not fall within a defined hardship area." I was amused, not surprised and would not have lived other than we did but wondered how AID could persuade its employees to learn about real conditions if they did not reward them for doing so up close. I was sufficiently supported, but such encounters quickened my sense that the practices, vision, and data of anthropology and those of business types and administrators are very different.

Had I been alert to the agency's sensitivities and politically cautious, I might have averted what could have been the termination of our stay. After a year of fieldwork, while George and I were meeting in Panama City, a friend of his, the journalist Charles Bartlett who was a Pulitzer Prize-winning national columnist and friend of President Kennedy, came through Panama City. George introduced us, and Bartlett interviewed me.

Without considering my funding source, I talked about the impoverished conditions in the countryside, the need for agricultural and subsistence help, and AID's lack of interest in directing aid to the rural folk. AID money in Panama, I explained, was devoted to building a new road from the airport to Panama City and a sewer system in the city seemingly to help the national economy grow. Then, I hinted at possible government corruption and dropped in a few comparisons to Vietnam.

Several weeks later Bartlett published the substance of my remarks in his nationally syndicated column, entitled "One Man's Key to Latin Success." His version of our conversation contained statements such as

> The gap which Steven Gudeman discovered between promises like the one at Punta de[l] Este to "modernize the living conditions of our rural population" and the actual isolation in which the peasants are enduring their poverty is ominous because it embraces a majority of the world's population in political tinderboxes from South Vietnam to Bolivia.
>
> Some 80 percent of American aid to Panama this year is directed into such totally urban projects as a highway around Panama City and a new road to the airport. These are monuments which entrench politicians who are corrupt and unresponsive in their dealings with the campesinos.
>
> Gudeman's accounts confirm suspicions that the American aid program under President Johnson has hardened into a crash effort to expand the statistics for exports and gross national product, to add substance to the status quo without concern for the inequities which it represents in these countries.
>
> Aid officials visit the area, enthuse at the strides that have been made, make modest promises of support, and are not heard from again.
>
> Gudeman, living perhaps closer to the campesinos over a long period than any educated man since Che Guevara, has untangled the sad, illogical roots to the passive outlook which causes them to resist change and persist in their misery.
>
> American aid cannot help because it all goes to the central government which makes no effort in their direction. (Bartlett 1967: 13)

I had not known Bartlett would write about our conversation, and I did not see a draft of his column before its publication. When the article emerged in newspapers across the nation a few weeks after we talked, Roxane and I were in the United States and passing through New York where my parents lived. A telephone call came for me while I was in the elevator and I answered on the emergency extension between floors. The State Department in Washington was calling, and a voice bawled at me, "You made us look bad. We can stop you from returning to Panama. How could you have said those things about AID, which is supporting you?"

I was worried, because the fieldwork was incomplete and my field notes were in Panama. Would all be lost? I was angry that the State Department thought it could control the travel of a citizen to another nation without an act of Congress or that it could influence Panama to declare me persona non grata. Standing there, with the telephone to my ear and cold sweat on my back, I did not deny my words and could only say, "I didn't see the column in advance."

We hung up and in a shaken voice I told Roxane that we might be staying in the United States. The threats came to naught, but I agreed to report to the AID group when I returned to Panama where I received a lecture about my inexperience, but I did not apologize.

George and I continued our discussions while I was learning more and more about local life. Sitting in the hot countryside we wrote *The Veraguas Report* for submission to AID in hopes of influencing the agency to focus on development in the countryside and boost local welfare. If the details and examples of the people's difficult living conditions came from me, the theme of the report—creating "engines of change"—came from George, a subject he later developed into a book. After I left the country, the Business School published our report. If I had hopes of influencing the government's bureaucracy, they were quashed when AID, on seeing the report, required us to retrieve the distributed copies and insert a paper inside the front cover denying its approval of our suggestions. Their preface stated, "The findings, conclusions, and recommendations contained in it are those of the authors and not of the United States Government or any of its agencies." At least we had struck a discordant note with their way of approaching development.

In addition to the booklet I produced with Lodge, I participated in a local group, headed by a member of the church, which produced a pamphlet called *Plan de Veraguas*. With some photographs by Roxane and a preface by Bishop McGrath, it emerged shortly after I finished my fieldwork. The report provided an overview of local conditions and the cooperative movement in Veraguas. Both it and the report with Lodge had unforeseen consequences a few years later.

Development work for AID was only part of my project for the Business School. The second task was producing a teaching case for a new business school in Guatemala that the Harvard Business School was helping to organize at the request of President Kennedy. Lodge was involved. Because I had chosen to study a village that had just begun to raise sugarcane for sale to one of the local mills that crushed it for the production of sugar, I thought a business case about the relation between the peasant growers and the mill would be a new type of case and very appropriate for use in Latin America. It turned out to be more than that.

Through connections that Lodge generated, I met with the head of the mill, who was also the vice president of Panama. His family owned the mill, while the family of the prior president owned the other mill to which the peasants also sold their sugarcane. When I met the vice president in Panama City, he agreed to the study and directed me to speak with the manager of the mill located about fifty minutes from the village.

The manager was a Cuban émigré. He told me about the mill's procedures and its relation to the local peasants but would not reveal its financials, although I deduced most of them. Profits looked to be more than US$1 million per year, which was considerable at the time and for the country.

The manager and other administrators were straightforward and matter-of-fact about the tasks of supplying seed to the campesinos and paying them for their sugarcane when it was brought to the mill for grinding and refining. But as one said, "The campesinos are uneducated and lazy, which complicates getting the raw cane." Another administrator added, "The local growers should take more responsibility for their lives and try to advance." He did not explain what advancing meant or how it would happen given the poor resource base, the lack of funding for agricultural improvements and the weak educational program available to the people. "That is not our responsibility," one administrator told me.

The peasants were sometimes resentful of the mill but felt powerless to do much about the situation. As one person sagely observed, "The mill saved us by providing money for the sugarcane, and they ruined us by destroying the land and forest for growing our crops." The mill's management knew about the poverty of the peasants yet did not "see" that their million-dollar yearly profit was connected to the people's continuing impoverishment. As my larger picture of economy developed, I interpreted the mill's view that its suppliers were irresponsible and lazy as a rationalization for its much higher salaries and comfortable profit. Their story validated their takings.

With this double-sided information, I put together a leery case about this sugar firm that sold its product in Panama and the United States but faced a complicated supply situation. I thought the case was written for the new Central American business school, but it went to Cambridge where the Harvard Business School used it as the final exam in its required first year course. It would have been difficult for me to solve the case in a business acceptable way, because I thought more money should have gone to the peasant workers at the cost of the mill's bottom line. For a number of years, I received notice from the Business School that I had written a best seller.

***

The largest part of my time in Panama was devoted to anthropology. When I had returned to Cambridge, England—after the summer in Panama and before the intensive fieldwork—to catch up in the discipline and present my PhD plans, everyone was impressed by my proposed project to study agricultural decision-making by constructing decision trees, attaching outcomes to each branch and multiplying these by their probabilities to find the returns a campesino could expect by following one or another arm of the tree. Then, I had only to compare the people's actual selections to the ideal routes and to each other. I learned the methodology, new to anthropology at the time, at the Business School and thought it would be easy to explore the people's yearly choices among growing rice, maize, and sugarcane.

To my consternation, when I tried to use decision tree analysis in the first days of arriving in the village, my two neighbors to whom I went had no idea what I was asking. "I seed enough rice to last for a year, and then add some beans and maize to the rice in the field," said one. "I don't work for money," responded the other.

In the many months following, I often went to one or the other of these men for quick responses to questions I might later develop. They were always helpful. Roberto, who had a ten-year-old daughter, was rather quiet. Slim and in his thirties, he was always neatly dressed with a clean shirt tucked into his pants unless he had just finished working in the fields. Even if impoverished, like everyone else, Roberto seemed to manage his life well with his mate and daughter. He would answer my occasional questions in an organized way that I appreciated. I seldom saw him socialize with others.

The other neighbor, Virgilio, also friendly, had a considerable stammer that made him difficult to understand. Short and never neatly dressed, he had a number of siblings and half-siblings in the village and was no longer an assiduous worker. Known in the village as the "rabbit" for his fecundity, Virgilio and his mate produced several children during our stay, and I was told he had had relations with other women in the village.

Both our neighbors gave me similar responses to my questions about decision-making. Neither thought in terms of probabilities and money outcomes, and their answers, I later found, reflected what others said and did. Constructing decision trees may work in business or on Wall Street, but my project was going to be useless in the countryside unless I trained the people to think like a business school graduate.

I jettisoned the crafted plan and then was lost. I had to learn something about the people's life but now did not know what to look for. At Cambridge, anthropologists focused on the "social structure" of a group, which was said to be the backbone of people's lives. Most of that work was carried out in Africa and attended to the way lineages, traced through males or females, were organized, which is why I had been admonished to study that drier aspect of anthropology. As those studies accumulated over several decades, the variations in the presumed structures increased and became ornate, and sometimes the data from the field did not fit the ideal plan that anthropologists had worked out. These studies did not help me because in the Panama countryside there were no lineages based on a string of females or males. The people did not remember more than two generations of ancestors, and nothing was written down. At Cambridge, religion, ritual, politics, and law were important to study, but they were seen in light of the presumed patrilineage or matrilineage that provided the spine of social life. Since that time the focus on lineage has almost been abandoned because the lineage could be an invention of the anthropologist who wanted to show that the studied society had a lasting structure.

Even searching for an enduring structure of kin relations was not useful in Panama. The village consisted of ninety-one small family houses that did not last as a group beyond the nuclear family. Couples also broke apart, people moved within and between villages, children sometimes lived with someone other than their parents, and men occasionally denied their paternity. The houses, which were usually made of sticks lashed together with vines, swamp grasses for a thatch roof and sometimes dried mud for walls, fell apart if not tended. Where was the backbone of social life for which I had been taught to look?

Other topics for study did not seem promising. Provincial and national authorities held political power and maintained little contact with people in the countryside, except at election time when politicians bought votes for money, alcohol, or the promise to build a water pump.

I was at a dead end, but that turned out to be a blessing. I had to become a hands-on anthropologist and learn about the people's life. Within a few days, I began walking about the village, watching people, introducing myself and talking with them. When I visited a house, the occupant, usually a woman at home, offered a small cup of coffee made by boiling the grounds over a wood fire. Local watching worked in the other direction. I was on show, and people knew where Roxane and I went and peeped inside our dwelling.

One day early during fieldwork, a woman said, "I saw you visiting Domingo. How is his sick child?" A few days later I heard, "What were you doing in the lagoon area on Thursday?" Children walked into our house, sometimes when I was naked. If we loaned money to someone, others knew.

I decided to learn about the people's agriculture, and bought a machete with the intention of going to the fields, helping and watching. After one man showed me how to sharpen the machete on a stone (he did it), I went with him and others to his field and tried to help chopping down branches and trees in preparation for the yearly cycle. My aim was poor, the work was tiring, and I told myself that I was there for other purposes. A few said, "He's trying," and someone added, "like a campesino."

I learned about slash-and-burn agriculture in the succeeding months. Each man tried to have 10–15 hectares of forest and scrub in reserve. At the start of the dry season, he located a patch of growth, cut it down using a machete or sometimes an axe, and left it to dry in the hot sun. Then, with the help of others, he set fire to the dried wood. After using the patch for two years, he would leave it for ten to fifteen years so the forest regenerated.

I participated in the fire setting, which was usually done at night when the wind was not so strong. A path around the area of downed wood was cleared by machete. A few men would start the fire with burning branches on a side chosen so the wind would blow the flames across the field. The breeze often changed direction, and I would hear great whoops as men ran around the burning field to keep the blaze from leaping the firebreak. Accidents happened. Once we helped a woman who was frantically throwing water on her thatch roof to smother threatening sparks. Some years later, when I was returning by small airplane from the rain forest on Panama's North Coast, we passed over the midsection of the country at the end of the dry season. As we traversed the central provinces, I saw smoke rising in one area and then another, giving signs of the shared practice at the start of the agricultural cycle.

Intrigued by the laborious preparation of the land and use of fire, I decided to continue learning about this way of raising crops. It was strange to me. I am not a farmer, do not keep a garden, and hate to mow grass or sweep outside wherever we live, but in Panama I went to the fields, watched, talked, and recorded. On 15 June 1966, after one field had been burned and the brush cleared, I wrote,

> We walked back to Pablo's land where he was seeding about a hectare. He had five people working for him. Two of the men went ahead and made holes in the ground with a *chuzo*. The *chuzo* is a long stick, taller than a man. Thick and weighty, it is sharpened to a point at one end. As he walks, a man has only to raise the stick and drop it to the ground to make a hole. The holes are about three inches deep and two feet apart. One man walks along making a row of holes that is not really a straight line but weaves slightly from side to side. The work is done slowly, because it must be carefully done, they told me. The other men and women plant the rice. Each worker has a short stick and a half gourd filled with rice. They put five or six seeds in a hole, then use the stick to fill in some dirt. The gourd usually is held in the left hand and the seeding is done with the right. The stick is held and used with the right, too. They walk bent at the hips with their legs spread a little apart to make the bending easier. It is not done bending the knees. People seem to work at least ten minutes without straightening up. It is not easy. Once the rice has been seeded, Pablo will plant beans in about half the land. In July he will put in sugarcane when the rice and beans have emerged. He was not seeding maize in the field as some others do. Pablo gave me some figures about his seeding and projected harvests.

After the seeding, everyone is hoping the yearly rains quickly arrive. When the rice and maize eventually emerge, they must be weeded. Lacking herbicides, the people cut the weeds with a machete by trimming around the base of each clump of rice. Bending at the waist and often at the knees, a worker moves through the field cutting the unwanted growth. Time-consuming and tiring, weeding is done twice if not more during the growing season. If sugarcane, the cash crop the people grow, is planted among the home crops, it is weeded with them.

This early stage of my fieldwork did not seem valuable and was not stimulating. I was watching and asking questions about agriculture. People were friendly and helpful, but I could not see where my work was leading other than to dull observations. I had ample time for more study but was struggling because I could not see any purpose to the fieldwork.

My feelings began to change as I followed the agricultural cycle to its end. At the rice harvest, the worker cuts the stalks at their base with a machete and gathers them into a "fistful," which he puts down. Three fistfuls are then tied together to make a "handful," which is the unit for figuring how much a field yields and the amount a house needs for the year.

Seeing these two measurements, I became fascinated by the way the human body was deployed as a measurement device in agriculture. The men used arm lengths or walking paces to gauge the land area to be seeded by one person. Stretching both arms perpendicular to the body and pacing sideways to make a square of sixteen arm lengths measured a day's work of weeding. Objects at hand also were used for measurements. Half a gourd held the amount of rice grains needed to seed several rows in a hectare, and numerous gourds measured a day of work, although the gourds differed in size.

The body was a convenient tool in other ways. When speaking about someone, a person seldom said the name or pointed with an arm or finger in her direction, especially when criticizing. The head was turned in the direction of the person or his house, and the chin was raised and jerked slightly forward. When men talked about rice, the basic food eaten three times a day, they bent one arm, placed the other on its bicep and said with satisfaction, "Oomph, rice gives strength."

After the rice is harvested, the grain, which is still on the clumps of stalk, is stored in the rafters of the kitchen to dry and for safety from rodents. Each day women prepare the rice for eating. In front of the house, a woman knocks the seeds off their stalks into a three-foot high, large wooden mortar. Hefting a heavy wooden pestle, she cracks the shells of the seeds and then sorts through the pile clearing out the stalks, shells, stones, and debris. Periodically she throws the rice upward to let other debris waft away while the rice grain falls back into the mortar.

She soaks and soon cooks the rice on the raised kitchen hearth, made of stones and heated by wood gathered by machete. Watching the way adults and children eagerly ate rice made me hungry for it, even though I do not like rice. Preparing it provided satisfaction to women, they said to me, but I never measured those hours of daily work, because they are interspersed with other tasks. Even men said that women's work is more continuous, if dispersed, and longer than theirs.

When the maize is ready for harvesting, the worker walks along the rows, tearing off the ears and throwing them into a basket that is fashioned from vines and strapped to his back. The basket, made by other campesinos and purchased in markets, measures the amount of maize a field yields, although baskets are unequal in size. I bought one, and after fifty-five years of use as my wastebasket, it shows signs of wear.

When I saw how the maize is used, I became aware of the many ways the people were thrifty and make do. After the leaves are stripped, and the kernels are cut off and crushed to meal, the cob is kept to serve as a bottle top, to start a fire for the daily cooking or to use as toilet paper. Maize leaves become brushes for washing dishes and clothes or wraps for cooking the corn meal. The husk also is used to bundle the hard brown sugar cakes a few people make at home by grinding the cane stalks, cooking the raw juice and pouring it into wooden molds for drying. Seeing these and other practices, the skills of being thrifty and using leftovers became a theme in my understanding of the way a house economy works.

After leaving Panama, I learned more about the ecology of slash-and-burn farming. Contrary to traditional thought, and compared to machine agriculture, it can be ecologically efficient and conservative. The fallow period, when the forest regenerates, restores the soil with nitrogen, a nutrient rice and maize both deplete, while the ashes from the burned trees, which absorbed nutrients during their growth, also fertilize the land. The people told me much the same. When I asked about using commercial fertilizer, they responded that ash from the burned trees was their fertilizer and did not cost money. I did not think about the economy in ecological terms at the time, but recalled these and other practices when I turned to capitalism and its use of resources.

Two decades after this fieldwork I saw the same practice of slash and burn in the mountains of Colombia, with comparable ideas about it, and this form of agriculture is practiced in many parts of the world with different techniques and beliefs. As for the machete, the central tool, whenever I visit a marketplace, whether in Panama, Colombia, Guatemala, Kyrgyzstan or elsewhere, I look at the spread of tools on sale. Machetes are made in all parts of the world and vary in remarkable ways. Some are short and some are long, some have a thin blade and others are wide. In Panama people sharpen a machete on a stone, and if the blade breaks, they make the implement shorter. The machete can be used to cut down a tree, lop off a branch, cut a pineapple off its stem, harvest sugarcane, weed around a plant, dig a hole, or kill a snake. The Panamanian men carried one wherever they went. I wanted to bring several machetes home but knew I would be stopped at the airport.

Starting with the machete, I became curious about tools. In other places, I have looked at old iron and steel plants and their remnants, at sugarcane presses powered by horses, at the way bricks are differently fired for disparate purposes, at waterfalls with turbines at their base that drive a conveyor belt, at old coal mining operations, and at other mechanical processes. Historians, anthropologists, economists and others have written about the evolution of tools. I read these accounts but they usually bore me. I have wanted to uncover a theory about tools in relation to economy that says more than they save labor and are efficient. Tools, at least the ones I have looked at, are an extension of the body, such as the digging stick, hoe, and machete. Arms become levers, the body is the energy source, and the human is physically close to the growing plant or object. I imagined developing a language or grammar about the way tools are constructed and used, and have since enjoyed the thought but not its practical success.

This initial interest in tools, however, slowly led in a more fruitful direction, for I was learning more than the techniques of agriculture and the use of tools, although I did not realize it at the time. Sometimes a man would take me to see his growing rice that was swaying in a light wind. Stopping, he would say, "Isn't it pretty." I did not know how to respond, except to agree, for it was not what I thought was a beautiful view. I would hear the same comment about a fishnet someone had made or a house that had just been built or reconstructed. In contrast, a few physical views I thought were pretty did not seem to be noticed by the people. Only over the years did I begin to understand their comments, especially after watching craftsmen in Guatemala decades later. Even then, I thought of what was being done and how it was done as a form of "artisanship," perhaps akin to art. I might have hastened my understanding of economy if I had used the word "workmanship" or "craftsmanship" for the way Panamanians made leather sandals, built a house, processed rice after it was harvested, or wove a hat, whether done by females or males. People varied in their skills, of course, and there was a degree of "drudgery" in the work—at least, I assumed so—but there was pleasure in the doing and in doing it well. I was, at the time, thinking of work as irksome to be done quickly and done only to have food. I began to inch from this view years later after reading Thorstein Veblen's *The Instinct of Workmanship* (1922) and thinking about both the pleasure and the drudgery of doing anthropological fieldwork, which is a handicraft.

***

Producing and preparing food was only part of the people's material life, which I increasingly saw was a mixture of activities. Most people lived in two-room houses. Kitchen walls were made of upright thin poles lashed together by vines on a wooden frame, which allowed air to blow through and eyes to look out. For bedroom walls, mud was plastered on a wooden lattice or sugarcane leaves were tightly layered on it. Families slept together in the bedroom on wooden beds. The roof that covered both rooms was made from thatch or long rushes lashed to a wooden frame. Houses required constant upkeep. Going to the forest or swamp area and cutting the needed resource with a machete provided the material for the repairs, and sugarcane leaves were used to fill holes in walls.

Some people kept small gardens for growing yuca, medicinal plants to make teas, bananas, papayas, avocadoes, clumps of sugarcane for chewing, and spices all of which became occasional additions to the regular fare. Chickens reserved for eating on festal days wandered in and out of most houses eating scraps and occasionally laying an egg. Furniture was made of roughly cut wood. Sandals were fashioned by hand from purchased leather, and everyone wore a straw hat that some women wove from strips of cane. In the past people made their clothes, although by our time clothing was store-bought and repaired at home.

When men were not working in the fields, they fished or hunted, although infrequently. Some occasionally sought paid work for a dollar a day in the village or a neighboring one. A few made items for sale from fishnets to horse blankets made of reeds.

Securing food, cooking it, and doing other needed tasks required a large portion of the day. It contrasted with the brief time Roxane and I spent buying and cooking spaghetti on our two-burner propane stove and adding canned tuna. When I was in Panama City, people would tell me "campesinos are lazy and careless." Our neighbors put more effort into surviving than most city employees and ourselves.

The fronts of two houses in the village were turned into small stores that sold necessities, such as salt, cooking oil, coffee in small packets, small cans of food, kerosene for lamps fashioned from old oil cans, and batteries for transistor radios. Both product sizes and store inventories were small. A packet of coffee grounds, cooked in hot water, made about three cups and cost one-twentieth of the daily wage when earned. It was infrequently drunk, and usually reserved for visitors.

Soap operas and the twice-weekly lotteries were popular radio shows. One neighbor told me, "I listen to boxing on the radio."

"Have you seen a fight?" I asked.

"No, I imagine it," he answered.

Another day I heard a young woman singing "Laura's Tune" from the recent film *Dr. Zhivago*. The music had reached the airwaves. At noontime and shortly after, people could send a message by radio to someone in the countryside and hope that a neighbor would relay it. Listening by battery power was costly, however. Most people did not listen all day, placed their batteries in the sun to preserve them and often purchased their radios over time. In fact, even radios had been owned by villagers for less than ten years.

One village store had a small, kerosene refrigerator and sold cold Coca-Colas. Occasionally I saw a man drinking one or taking it home to share with his family. A Coke cost ten cents or 10 percent of the daily wage when earned, so his purchase was an extravagance and deviation from the people's thriftiness. I sympathized; the drink provided quick energy and relief in the heat but could cause trouble given the cost and the needs of his house. I speculated that Coke must have a universally inviting taste that crosses cultures. Then, I wondered if sugar from a person's sugarcane field ever came back to him in one of the bottles he drank. Was this a circle of extraction? When harvesting sugarcane, a man earned $1.25 per day, and he and his family could not survive on 12.5 bottles of Coke each day.

***

Roxane turned to her research on children's language learning. She drew marvelous pictures of the children's activities, designed questions about them, and recruited young children of different ages to respond (often with their mothers present). Sitting at a small table in our house she focused on grammar acquisition and mistakes, which fitted her interest in cognitive development. Taping their answers for later statistical analysis, she accumulated the data for her PhD. She also interviewed mothers about their beliefs concerning children and child-rearing and collected traditional stories told by both children and adults.

My interest in language was not so organized. I struggled to understand what the people were doing in agriculture and the words for their activities. I watched, listened, and made notes but had no way of framing what was happening.

Ten years after fieldwork I began to see the men's agricultural language as figurative or metaphoric. They used barbering terms when working in the fields. A man "sheared" a field of its stubble for planting. Later he "cut" the weeds around his plants directly on top of the land or "broke the casing of the earth's head" when severing them at their roots. As I looked more closely at their words, I realized they were talking about the meaning of their labor in relation to the land. Like barbers they "picked off" the harvest. Their work in the fields was necessary to secure food, but their many efforts in the field did not make the crops grow any more than a barber causes hair to be longer. Their words seemed to undercut our notion that labor is "productive." At the time, I concluded they believed that labor did not add "value" in production, but I could not fit their idea to any larger understanding beyond the idea that their vision did not fit ours, and I could not explain farming as a form of barbering. Only years later after fieldwork in Colombia and an exploration of early ideas in economics did I reach an understanding of their figurative language.

One difference between our ideas about economy bewildered me, but its resolution, if later obvious, became an important component in my mental toolkit. One Sunday afternoon, I was chatting with Roberto, our neighbor, when he confused me with his measuring scales. We were sitting on low stools in front of his mud house talking about rice and sugarcane. As I listened and took notes on my clipboard, he kept switching measuring rods between physical ones and money. I was puzzled, because the sugarcane is seeded and weeded in the same field with the rice. When I asked him again and then again why he switched the measuring rod for the two crops, he kept repeating what he had said.

> A task for weeding rice is measured by walking sideways for sixteen steps with arms held out to make a square. The work may be completed in a day, in less than a day or in more than a day. A half gourd measures the volume of seed needed for several rows in a rice field. The harvest is measured by handfuls and stored on the stalk above the hearth for eating. The workers come from my house and are not paid, or I exchange labor with someone else in the village.

I had seen these practices and understood what Roberto was saying, but these physical measures disappeared when he talked about sugarcane. Once the rice is harvested, a number of workers come to the same field, slice each stalk of sugarcane at its base and strip its leaves with a machete. He continued:

> The worker carries a bunch of the stripped cane on his shoulder to a ten-ton truck that is driven onto the field and the load is transported to one of the mills. At the mill, the sugarcane owner, who travels with the driver, goes to the back of the truck and takes two stalks from the top of the load, two from the middle, and two from the bottom, carefully picking ripe ones. The truckload is weighed, the truck's weight is subtracted and the sugar content of the selected stalks is sampled. Using this sample, the mill calculates the amount of sugar that can be

> extracted from the entire truckload and pays cash for it at the end of the week to the owner of the field. The owner pays the trucker and each worker for his days of labor, although not for the volume of cane that each cut and loaded.

I could not make sense of what I was hearing from Roberto about these different payments, because my financial mind kept asking, "Why do the people use disparate measures for the two crops? Why not value rice by the money it could bring if sold or by the cost of purchasing the same amount that is harvested, and then divide one of these sums by the labor used to produce it in order to figure the value of a day's labor in rice? The measurement systems differ, but the same field is used for both crops, and the land preparation and the weeding serve both crops."

Ten years later, when I came back to these notes, I saw that Roberto was speaking about the difference between a nonmonetary economy, typified by the rice calculations, and a monetary economy exemplified by the sugarcane calculations. Then, I saw that the two systems could be in conflict, and a few years later entitled a book *Economy's Tension* to designate the conflict between making material life through unpaid relationships, as in raising rice for the house, and making material life through money and markets as with the sugarcane. Finally, I understood my conversation with Roberto on a Sunday afternoon in Panama.

Even with this foretaste of a different way of thinking about economy, I remained imbued with money ideas during fieldwork and often posed market questions to the people. When I asked one man about profit, he answered, "We don't think about that." Another said, "It is a puzzle. We think of working to eat, to get enough for next year, to live. Nothing more. We don't go along adding up money bills."

Sometimes my questions led in unexpected directions. The older term for barter or swap, one person told me, is *cambalache*. "Now people say, *cambiar* (change or exchange). We exchange (*cambiar*) chickens and a machete. But if we take someone else's woman, we say *cambalache* a woman." Use of the word had become sardonic, referring not to swapping goods but to partner taking.

Answers to my questions could be contradictory. When I spoke with Miguel about borrowing, he replied, "Certainly, we borrow money, tools, and food." He talked about people who loan and do not loan to others and explained, "He who has friends can always borrow, and he who does not have friends cannot borrow." Then, Miguel added a phrase I heard several times. "He who does not have friends cannot borrow. He is not a person." Miguel, I realized, meant that exchanging back and forth makes relationships and a place in community. Refusing to borrow and loan severs that sociability.

When we returned to the topic a month later, however, Miguel said, "It is embarrassing to borrow from others." Reciting his earlier statement, I said, "Isn't that contradictory?" He responded, "Yes, I cannot explain it."

***

Borrowing and exchanging took a different form with the *junta*, which is a collection of people helping someone with a large task. I watched *juntas* for harvesting and helping to build or move a house. Jacinto, an energetic man I often visited, held a major house-building *junta*. On one side of his house, he had an open counter for a store, tended by his partner, Eugenia. Their sleeping quarters and kitchen were in the rear. Now, Jacinto wanted a separate house for their bedroom and decided to hold a *junta*.

He spent weeks planning the structure, inviting participants, and collecting materials that included shaved poles for holding a lattice for the walls. He collected straw and piles of clay, and his father brought sand and huge drums of water in his oxcart. A few days in advance, Jacinto's partner arranged with other women to make the alcoholic maize drink, *chicha*, to be served to the men whom Jacinto had invited to help several weeks in advance. Some of them owed him a day of house building from years past. Others he would owe in the future.

The day began early. Men gathered and began to stomp the dirt, sand, straw, and water into a muddy mixture to plaster onto the wooden frame. I joined. Back and forth we went in a line with arms over each other's shoulders. Their hardened soles equipped them for the task. My feet were cut, and my legs were sore for days afterward. The wet mixture we created was carried in clumps to the frame where others plastered it on the lattice. It all had to be done in a day, because the mud dries overnight.

Jacinto directed the activities and went from one task to another, assisting as needed. As the day proceeded, we were served the *chicha*, and at midday we all took a break for plates of rice and beans that had been cooked by several women who were helping. The pace of work slowed after midday and tempers quickened. In the afternoon, a fight broke out between Mario and Jaime who were arguing over a debt. It was impossible to understand what they were saying as both had been drinking large quantities of *chicha*. I held Mario's arms back while others separated the two. Then, both began to cry but more from the drink than the hurt.

Late in the day, when we were finishing, several men began uttering a celebratory howl from deep in their throats. Known as *gritando* (shouting or yelling), the howl sounds like a wolf's cry. Facing one another and taking turns, they yowled, but hardly in tune. Roxane took pictures through the day, and at the end I went back to our house, cleaned my feet, and went to sleep.

Over the next days Jacinto put on the tile roof himself, and I returned to find out about the obligations he had incurred. I asked why he served so much drink and provided endless quantities of food. He replied, "If you don't do that, they won't come." The *junta* is celebratory work, I soon recognized, and different from the frequent exchanges of labor between two men or among a group of men who work one another's fields. The *junta* never involves cash payments, and the obligation to return the labor can stretch for a decade or more, if finally paid.

***

Even with these accumulating experiences I could not form an overall picture of the local economy. I did not even have a clear view of what I meant by economy, as our standard ideas and expressions—rational choice, calculated exchange, the uses of money, and investment—did not work. I kept collecting information because I knew nothing about agriculture or living from the land, and I was groping for a handle.

Lacking a framework for what I saw, I was forced to be open to happenings and to the people's words. Every day I typed an account about what I observed and what people said. I had a portable Olivetti typewriter and typed slowly due to my inept fingers and the lightweight machine. These daily notes had no divisions or topical headings. I typed them in triplicate using carbon paper. The third copy was a paper-sized, stiff, yellow Royal McBee, "Keysort" card. Later, during focused interviews I took handwritten notes and shortened the daily accounts.

The Keysort cards had numbered holes running around their four edges and came with a tool for punching out a hole's outside edge and a long needle for threading through a hole. To use the cards, I had to specify a topic, give it a number, and go through the cards punching the outside edge of the numbered hole for that topic when it appeared on a card. When I wanted to explore a topic that I had created and punched, I only needed to push the needle through its numbered hole in a stack of cards, hold the needle horizontally and the punched cards would fall. Each card had 170 numbered holes, and combinations of the numbered holes could be used to add categories and subcategories. The possibilities seemed endless with this 1960s technology. The thought that this new tool would heighten my analytical ability and raise my productivity helped motivate me to watch, talk, and type every day.

After fieldwork, I went through the day notes and tried to devise categories for sorting but was quickly stymied. Each typed card contained material that could be classified in different ways. Was a simple task like seeding part of economy, production, labor, ritual, the weather, the household, gender, age, or consumption? Did I need to distinguish the type of seed and how long it took to mature? Should I code whether a group or a single person did the seeding? The possibilities were indeed endless, and the task was daunting, especially since seeding was a very minor part of my observations. I was caught in a vicious circle. Until I analyzed the material, I did not know what categories to specify, and once I had the categories I already would have organized the material. I quit this method of analysis after a few frustrating days.

Typing the daily notes, however, helped fix in my mind occasions and words on which my eventual interviews focused, and they provided immediate accounts about people, ceremonies such as baptisms and funerals, social life, and the local economy. Few of my later formal interviews concerned economic life, because I had many details in the day notes.

If research involves searching for a foothold, anthropology provides the extreme example. I asked questions of people because I did not understand what they were doing or saying. Even when they explained and repeated their words, I often did not grasp the meanings or how what they said fit with anything else. What did it mean that rice "gives strength" and that the earth "gives strength to the rice," or that "helping" means sharing your "strength"? I was not trying to keep an open mind. The questions came because I did not like feeling utterly lost.

Anthropologists talk about culture shock or the disorientation felt when moving to a strange culture. The discomfort and loneliness disappear as the new food, language, and customs become familiar. In Panama my discomfort was different. I often recalled the psychological idea of "cognitive dissonance," which is the feeling of mental disorientation when beliefs or ideas clash or do not fit together.

As soon as I began to grasp one part of the people's economy, such as the agricultural cycle, another ill-fitting part came to me. No anthropologist had provided an alternative way of thinking about economy that helped me, and my knowledge of business economy did not explain their material life. Were people maximizing, as I had been taught to do in the Business School? If so, in agriculture were they maximizing the amount of the rice or maize or beans they grew? Were they maximizing or minimizing the labor they did? Besides, I did not even hear the word "maximize" or a comparable term while in Panama. For agriculture the people seemed to figure what they needed for eating in the coming year, which could be an instance of "satisficing" (as some economists use the term) or accepting what they could do under constraints. They did want money, but the opportunities to secure it were limited. How could I describe their activities? Even the word "economy" was not used as a cover term for a domain of life. It seemed to mean being careful or thrifty in the use of material things or money, as in "economizing" or "making economies." Was I searching for a big picture that was not there? My cognitive dissonance lasted while I was in the field, was endlessly stressful, and continued after leaving Panama. I was watchful like any anthropologist, but I did not know if my trails led anywhere. Turning away from using decision trees in the early days of fieldwork had put me on this exasperating path.

***

My failure getting the people to think in terms of decision trees led to another unplanned part of the research. Because my Cambridge training in describing the enduring patrilineages or matrilineages of a people was completely useless, I had to turn to what was there. The village was a collection of houses formed around nuclear families. The houses seemed to be placed where people could find a small plot of land, and they were spread here and there, seldom in clusters, and over a large area sometimes near only a narrow path in the forest, scrub, or tall grass. Only some families lived near other family members, membership of a house changed, and occasionally houses were abandoned. Outsiders originally and the government's agrarian reform agency later owned the land, so the people never had legal rights to the plots they occupied.

I decided that if I could not find classic lineages or a permanent village structure, I could at least study families and kinship relationships. In my day notes for 14 June 1966, about six months into fieldwork, I grimly told myself, "Will have to begin on kinship soon. It certainly appears there are some kinship patterns." I was feeling sour, because my patience with the subject of kinship had been exhausted at Cambridge.

I soon found that kinship in the village was an endless series of connections that did not lead to the treasure chest of a final ancestor as in a lineage but spread endlessly up, down, and to the side, and then folded back on itself. Where was the structure? I wish I had approached the topic with humor rather than doggedness, because delightful surprises appeared. Over several days I wrote down a series of sibling ties that were typical:

- Emilio is a half-brother of Celestino by their mother,
- Celestino is a half-brother of Vicente, Segundo, Eugenia, and Delfin by their father,
- Vicente, Segundo, Eugenia, and Delfin are half-siblings of Bienvenido by their mother,
- Bienvenido is a half-brother of Anibal by their father,
- Anibal is a half-brother of Francisco by their mother, and so it went.

On the floor, I drew a huge kinship diagram of these connections linking everyone in the village. It went on and on to the sides with crossing links, as in the example (and not much vertically because the generations were short), but what did it tell me? I had never seen anything like this in the literature. I realized that I had to find out more about sexual and gender relationships, and their connections to parenthood, the family, and who was living with whom. Where were the neat rules I had been taught and wanted to find?

I first asked people how paternity and maternity were linked to sexual relations, because men often claimed, with a laugh, that they could always deny their paternity, although gossips sometimes pointed to the similarity of physical features between a man and his children. Everyone agreed that a woman could never deny her motherhood, because "she would always know, even if she gave birth in the bush." Contraceptive devices were not readily available, although some herbal abortifacients were said to be effective.

Part of the puzzle was finding out when paternity was and was not recognized by both men and women, and that question led me to the connection of paternity with age, the house, and living together. Julia, who I watched moving here and there, was known for her numerous sexual relationships. Carlos, in a lowered voice, told me that she had refused to sleep with Cruz because she had slept with his father. I did not know if she actually had been intimate with Cruz's father, or directly ask her, but her denial (according to the story) helped illuminate local concepts. Coupling with him, she told Cruz, would be like having sex with a stepchild. A stepfather, people agreed, should not sleep with a stepdaughter if she had lived with him in his house before she reached puberty. Julia's refusal of Cruz illustrated local reasoning when gender-reversed, age-stretched, and co-residence overlooked.

Drawing on accounts from others, I began to understand that paternity had to do with physical conception plus the two living in the same house and eating the same food together before the child reached puberty. Julia and Cruz had never lived in the same house and shared food, but her denial drew on these concepts. I still did not understand the reasoning until twenty years later, and after fieldwork in the related cultural situation of Colombia, when I grasped the local idea of "strength." Sharing the same food, which provides strength for life, connects people through the needed component for existing. This was the missing piece explaining Julia's denial of Cruz in Panama.

Despite this restriction on an adult male coupling with a young female after they had lived and eaten together, men lasciviously invoked the double *entendre*, "Raise your own pigeon so you can eat it." I was told that one such coupling occurred, although the age at which the girl lived with her stepfather and eaten the same food was fuzzy and was said to have taken place in a distant village.

Because I did not completely understand these and other accounts, they led me to look more closely at family relationships in the house. I was curious about sleeping arrangements. Parents and children share the small, completely enclosed bedroom that is never opened to outsiders. Trying to be an intrepid anthropologist, I asked about sexual relations of parents given the immediacy of their children. Parents are "circumspect," I was told. I was not satisfied, because the response raised another issue.

"If parents are circumspect," I asked, "why don't two adult couples or parents and a child with her partner share a house and bedroom? Everywhere only a couple with or without children live in a house."

"Two couples in the same house would hear each other," Carlos answered. His response contradicted the idea that parents were circumspect in the bedroom.

Eventually, I saw another reason why two couples do not share a bedroom or kitchen. It is the flip side of their aphorism, "the man is for the fields and the woman is for the house." Male and female are dependent on each other and each is "respected" for helping to make the house economically independent. If the two require another adult pair in the house to maintain it, others do not respect them.

Respect, I discovered, was a verbal honor and almost a currency. I never fathomed all its uses and meanings, although I asked question after question, and made notes and notes in hopes of writing it up. One had to respect God, godparents, people in power, and a person for the contributions she makes to the house. Gossip was prevalent about the latter. We often heard, "He doesn't bring enough home. He doesn't work hard and does not respect his family." About one woman, someone disparagingly said, "She does not have a hot drink for him in the morning so that he has the strength to work. A woman has to get up early, get the fire going, and heat something for her partner, or she is not respecting him." Respect, I could see, was a relational idea and value about how people interacted in the house and larger village.

None of this information emerged of a piece, and the foray started only because I was puzzled about an incredible string of siblings and half-sibling connections that led me to gender relations and the recognition of parenthood, which steered me to who shared a bedroom. Finally, when I saw the reason that two adult couples do not share a bedroom meant more than being sexually circumspect but encapsulated gender expectations and respect, I began to grasp the local rationale why households in the village were largely formed around nuclear families.

I did not know if I got it right but should have recalled that on the train from London up to Cambridge I would pass by the Howard's End stop, the name of the novel in which E. M. Forster offers the famous phrase "only connect," which is valuable advice for anthropologists.

I never fully resolved why two-thirds of the pairings were common-law unions, termed *juntado*, about 30 percent were church marriages, and 5 percent were civil unions. I surmised from the people's elliptical explanations that the statistics had to do with the high cost of a church marriage, the lesser cost of a civil union, and the lack of cost for a common-law pairing all of which reflected the contrary desires of males and females. In a variation of their aphorism about the gender division of labor—"the woman is for the house, the man is for the fields"—men often said, "The woman is for the house, the man is for the street," which justified their roving. Men felt less tied down in a common-law union in which they had no legal obligations. They could rove or leave, especially if they refused to "recognize" a child at birth. The pressure to have a civil or religious union usually came from the female, which meant her children would be "legitimate." Recognition referred to legally acknowledged paternity outside marriage. Sometimes, women explained, "A church marriage is better in the eyes of the church," but men retorted, "married, tired," which in Spanish emerges rhythmically as *casado, cansado*.

Occasionally a woman, alone or with children, maintained a house and people said, "She wields a machete like a man," which I interpreted as a compliment about her work rather than a disparagement of her sexuality, although such talk was often filled with overtones.

Roxane and I separately heard about the physical abuse of females. The stories were similar if affectively different because we each heard them from a gender perspective. Alcohol had a role. One drama revolved about Jacinto and Eugenia. I knew when it began because I was to meet Jacinto New Year's morning, and he did not appear. That night Edith came by our house, sat at our table, and asked "Would you loan Eugenia some money so she can go to Panama City?"

Jacinto, Edith related, had been drinking on New Year's Eve with friends, and Eugenia did not like him drinking. Edith continued,

> When he returned in the morning and she said something, Jacinto hit her in the mouth, knocking her down in front of others at the counter [of the store they have at the front of their house]. Jacinto went to the back and fell sleep. Eugenia took her bedding, went to her father's house [in a neighboring village], and decided to leave for Panama City where she can stay with a woman for whom she once worked.

After an interval, Edith resumed, "Eugenia's father told her, 'Don't go,' because Eugenia helps her father and cares for her nephew and niece who live with her." Some of the women we knew also observed that Eugenia tended the store and chickens she and Jacinto have and cooked in addition to caring for the nephew and niece. She "makes savings, and he just spends money," one said.

Edith, always a fount of talk, had an explanation for the row. "Eugenia is jealous and thinks Jacinto finds other women." She added that when a man comes home drunk, his partner should stay quiet. Edith recalled the times her partner had hit her when she said something critical, but she stayed with him. At least once before, said Edith, "Eugenia fled to Panama City. Jacinto finally traveled there and convinced her to return."

In the next weeks we went to Puerto Rico where I had agreed to help train Peace Corps volunteers. When we returned, Eugenia had not come back, and the story was alive. By then, I had heard Jacinto's account. "I only pushed Eugenia and she sat down." He remembered nothing else. Now his head hurt. Others told us he was inquiring through acquaintances whether Eugenia had another man in Panama City.

Jacinto was in a fix. He was tending the store, taking care of Eugenia's nephew and niece to whom he was attached, and unable to care for his crops. He was paying young men to work his land, while he cooked and washed. On visiting him one day as I often did, he kept getting up to stir the rice pot and instructed Eugenia's nephew how to cook strips of meat. The store was a mixed blessing. It tied him to the house all day but provided some cash in lieu of food from the field. Usually animated, he was quiet, looked drawn, and said nothing about the situation. As Eugenia's leave lengthened, Jacinto talked about going to a sorcerer for potions that would entice her to come back.

News about this and other events often came in unexpected ways. One evening, several months after Eugenia left, I attended a school meeting for parents. Bored and in need of relief, I went outside to pee in the bushes. There, I met Rufino who was doing likewise. "Jacinto looks sad," Rufino said, "but Eugenia will return in March. She has four more weeks of work in Panama City. Then she will return." Still relieving myself, I asked him, "How do you know?"

He learned this news from Apolonia who had been in Panama City where she, too, had taken a domestic job for a brief period. Rufino's information was almost accurate, for on 26 February Eugenia returned to the house, and the news circulated. Six days later I spoke with Eugenia who told me she had left her belongings in Panama City with the family she knew. They told her to return if Jacinto hit her again.

The drama of Eugenia and Jacinto captured local talk for good reason. Its themes revolved about gender relations, male power, abuse, drinking, children, the plight of women and their support, and connections to Panama City. Everyone had a perspective, including Roxane and me, but we were in a quandary. Both of us sympathized with Eugenia but did not help her go to Panama City. I wanted to avoid any favoritism. My reluctance to assist, however, could have been seen as implicit support for Jacinto. I frequently visited and talked with him as he was always helpful and pleasant. On her return, Eugenia resumed good relations with us, and I did not hear of Jacinto getting drunk again.

***

In a group, my eyes flitted this way and that as greetings among godparents, godchildren and *compadres* flowed back and forth when people joined or passed on a path. Brothers and sisters, parents and children, and other family members might be called out by name but not by label. These related people addressed each other as *compadre* or *comadre, padrino* or *madrina, ahijado* or *ahijada* (co-parent, godfather or godmother, godson or goddaughter), depending on the gender of the person greeted. This collection of relationships is known as the *compadrazgo*.

People formed these ties over baptism, confirmation, and at a church marriage. Studies showed that godparent ties may be used to form connections to merchants, politicians, and wealthier people. A merchant may lower a price or provide a loan to his compadre, a politician may help his godchild find a job, and a wealthy person may provide gifts or connections to a compadre or godchild. The tone of these studies was matter-of-fact.

I found something different. Few people in the village had outside connections to wealthy or powerful compadres. Most godparents live in the village or a neighboring one but do not provide help to their compadres or godchildren. Godparents attend the baptism and funeral of a godchild but do not adopt or foster godchildren, and they do not offer religious instruction or take them to church. Compadres did not necessarily work together, and they did not ask each other for food or money for fear of not paying back, because failing to repay a debt would break the respect they must maintain. Even though the bonds, whether between godparent and godchild or between compadres, have no substantial utility, why were they unfailingly formed at baptism?

I slowly saw that the substance of the bonds lay in their recognition. Greeting a godparent, godchild, or compadre was deemed respectful and necessary. Men said they never trusted another male to be alone with their partner, but they trusted a compadre due to the respect the compadre had for him. Intimate words and advances not to speak of sexual relations destroyed that respect. Despite these explanations, I could not make sense of these ties that had no material grounding other than words and respectful behaviors.

Then I remembered that in other studies the *compadrazgo* was presented as a catalog of one-to-one ties. Anthropologists described the godparent-godchild bond and how it might be used and the relation between compadres and its material features, but the two were not connected or linked to other relationships. They looked like separate ties whose prevalence was hard to understand.

Late one rainy afternoon, sitting at my typewriter and finishing some notes about godparents, I suddenly had a different vision. The *compadrazgo* is not a collection of separate ties between godparent and godchild, and between parents and godparent but a set of relationships consisting of the parents, godparent and godchild modeled after the nuclear family, yet the *compadrazgo* seems to oppose and complete the household family. The nuclear family lives within a house. Godparenthood is formed between houses within the village. The "content" of the two sets is different as the material to the spiritual, but the child who is offspring in one and godchild in the other links the houses through the constellation of bonds.

Finally, I had found a village "structure" both in the British mode of real social relationships and in the more abstract mode of Lévi-Straussian structuralism in which relationships are defined not in themselves but in relation to other relationships, which in this case was almost a mirror reversal. I started saying to myself, "Alice in Wonderland," both for the mirroring of the two and for my own wonder at what was there, especially because prior examples of structuralism had all come from non-Western settings.

Then, I began to find behaviors and language that fit the pattern. A family tries to be independent economically through its material ties based on kinship. Godparenthood bonds consist of sacred ties that have no material features. In the family context the expression "hot hand," I recalled, refers to a man who has many children. He is sexually potent and provides life-giving strength. In the godparenthood set, "hot hand," I found, refers to a godfather whose godchildren die before him. From one to the other the meaning of male potency is reversed, and people spoke of not choosing a godfather with a "hot hand."

I found that an older sibling was never chosen to be godparent to a younger one if they lived in the same house, but if the older sibling had a separate house, he could serve as godparent to his younger sibling. Godparent choice had to go outside the house and so linked them.

Godparent choice also could not be reversed. If one person chose another to be godparent for his child, the selected godparent could not ask back or reverse the relation between the two houses. If choice were reversed, the people told me, the spiritual relationships would be undone. This irreversibility meant that choice had to go on and on among the houses in the area. Even if these religious ties in the village did not have an overall pattern, they supplemented those of the family in the house by providing a network of spiritual relationships in the community.

I had been trained to look for the social structure of a group of people. The family-godparenthood system in the outlands of Panama was unlike the lineages anthropologists purported to find in Africa and elsewhere, or anything else I had heard about but all the more satisfying for that.

***

After more than six months in the village, I began individual interviews with two men that I had spoken with several times. I had many questions about village life, although to speak of questions that needed answers overstates what I knew, for much of the people's life remained hazy to me and more was obscure.

I asked Carlos and Miguel to work with me, because their ages and experiences differed. I paid each slightly more than the daily wage ($1.00) for less than a day's work. When we first talked about the possibility of working with me, both were curious about what I was doing. All they knew was that I typed, watched, listened, and occasionally talked. Shortly after we started meeting at our house, each expressed concern about what others thought. "People asked what I was telling you," said Miguel after our initial discussions, but we never had problems.

Carlos, in his late thirties, was slight but energetic in his daily work and walked quickly. Rather quiet, he was observant and sometimes critical of others, but quick to understand what I was asking. He and his partner had a young son, who was sometimes teased by others his age, "Miguelito, *ratoncito* (little mouse)." Although Carlos's brother lived in the village and his mate had a few relatives there, he did not have many friends and sometimes seemed disconnected or uninterested in others. I never saw him chatting or playing dominoes in the evening. I trusted his answers, although on topics such as religion in which he took little interest, his responses were not expansive. I could ask him anything, which I did from costs to coition, and he was filled with bits of gossip given his observant and sometimes cynical nature. A bit of a braggart, he claimed to have slept with a hundred women (which I doubted).

Miguel represented a slightly different generation and outlook. He was in his fifties, and though he was not overweight, which would have been hard for anyone to achieve in the village, he was stubbier than Carlos. Miguel lived near several of his siblings and knew almost everyone in the village but like Carlos did not have close friends. His nature was decent, thoughtful, and cooperative but he was less verbally expressive than Carlos and not as incisive or as explanatory when responding to a question. Carlos was a diligent worker in his fields, but Miguel did not and perhaps could not apply himself in the fields or elsewhere in the same way.

Miguel was interested in local beliefs. Once, as we were talking, he spilled sparks from a tiny pipe onto his shirt and looked immediately at the burns to decipher them for a number on which he would bet in the weekly lottery. At times, he seemed the more thoughtful of the two men, for he often pondered a question before responding, though his answers were brief. Unlike Carlos, who could reach beyond a question that suggested new lines for me to follow, Miguel was less apt to grasp what I was trying to understand.

I prepared for the sessions with questions or issues for discussion, and used the same for each of them but shifted grounds when a question led nowhere or elsewhere. I never found marked discrepancies between what each told me and got along well with both.

Carlos and Miguel were not my only sources of information. I had amiable relations with others with whom I talked. Our closest neighbors were helpful, such as Alfredo who spoke about the different measures for the cash and domestic crops. Many days I walked around the village and talked with people at random. At night I might sit at a store watching men play dominoes while chatting with them, and I attended almost every ceremony, from baptisms to deaths, that took place. A few people wondered why I sat typing for hours during the day until others supplied the answer. It was my work.

After we departed Panama, Carlos left the village for the Darien jungle and fresh forest, because by that time the village land had passed to government control and was turned to raising only sugarcane. Carlos did not like being under the mill's control and wanted to raise his own food. Roxane had taken a photograph of Carlos seeding a rice field and another with his five-year-old son learning to work alongside him. The first picture appears on the cover of my second book (*The Demise of a Rural Economy*, 1978). Twenty years after the book was published, an anthropology student from Brown University contacted me to say she had spent time in the Darien area, had my book with her, and met a young schoolteacher who on seeing the cover, exclaimed "That's my father!" I wrote him with greetings and a gift for his dad. We were aware of possible negative reactions to taking pictures and sought permission before snapping them. The result with Carlos and his son was emblematic of the unpredictable world the anthropologist traverses.

During the interviews with Carlos and Miguel, I took notes by hand, which was quicker and less intrusive than typing. Each interview, conducted inside our house, lasted about three hours after which I spent more hours reviewing the notes, filling them out, adding side comments, thinking about new questions, and typing the separate day notes.

The interviewing was gender-biased, because I had to be careful. I would hear men say, "A man has license to do it even with his mother should he meet her in the street," adding "a woman has to defend herself." Their words reflected male conceit more than everyday reality, and I never heard examples of son-mother couplings even in folk tales, but a private interview with a lone woman at our house or elsewhere would have led to gossip and undermined my standing. The presence of Roxane or a woman's children helped legitimate interviews with females.

As Roxane continued her research on children's language acquisition, she expanded her long-time interest in photography taking pictures of village life and building a large collection of photos, some of which I used in publications. Talking with children and their mothers, she heard gossip beyond my ears. She listened to stories of spousal abuse ranging from black eyes to bruised arms. Some women told her about their desire to leave. She also talked with some men about child raising, for which I received ribbing.

During interviews I covered topics from the political order to religion and beliefs in addition to economy, the family, and godparenthood. The political situation at the local level continued to hold little interest for me, because town and city people held power. District representatives were usually aligned with national candidates, and votes were bought for money or a few promised amenities. The bishop told me about a representative in a neighboring province who spent $40,000 to win his contest and then felt he had the right to recoup the money, which he did through a government contract to finish a dirt road. The peasants told me how the voting process operated. A candidate would secure a batch of unmarked ballots in advance of the election. He paid helpers to mark and give them to voters, who hid them in their shirts. Substituting one for the other in the booth and then emerging, the voter handed over the clean ballot to be marked for the next person and received money or alcohol for his efforts.

***

After a year in the village, I devised a questionnaire about the economy of the house and tried it out on a few people. After revising it, I went for a bigger study. I wanted to include the ninety-one households in the village, so I took small pieces of paper and gave each house a number. We put the numbers in a bag and Roxane shook it for a long time to make the drawing random while I ached for an outcome sending me to people I knew or could easily reach on foot. I drew fifteen numbers one after another. We kept their order to have ten houses and five alternates. Some of the selectees I knew. Some were reasonably near, but others would be difficult to find in the distant forest and savannah, and I moaned. Some were only names, and some made me groan given their personalities. I started with trepidation. How could I ask people I hardly knew to answer strange questions?

The connected problem was finding the houses of the people selected, which led to another unintended finding about maps and history. There were no signposts, markings for paths, or other indicators showing where people lived or worked. When I asked, "Where does Jose live," someone would say, "North of green tree" or near "Juan's land." Neither answer was helpful until I realized people had a mental map, actually two mental maps, of the area. One map that I think of as the earlier one used place names, such a "green tree" and "deep pool" to designate about thirty hectares of the village area. By a different reckoning someone might say "Juan's house" or "Juan's land," which would be modified as "near green tree." To my dismay, there were not only many green trees and many deep pools in the village but the description was arbitrary. The physical feature did not always have a real-world referent in the landscape. Eventually, I grasped that the two maps were related to land claims and their changes over time.

The pictorial or nature map referred to some environmental features and to the people's relationship to the land. The land for houses and agriculture belonged to none of them (it had been held by absentee owners who never visited or used it), and so was occupied by anybody to build a house. Forested land was used for a year or two before it needed to be left fallow for about ten years in order to regenerate trees and scrub for the slash and burn agricultural cycle. By the time we arrived, usable forested land was becoming scarce as the population had grown. The absentee owners, whose family had been rewarded with the land on the independence of the New World from Spain, always had lived in Panama City. Years before, they wanted to sell it to an outsider, who tried to evict all the people (which led to an armed struggle in which one man died). Eventually, the agrarian reform agency purchased all the land but did not distribute it. Now, land claims for agriculture against others in the village were made by using a plot within a larger claimed area, and these claims were enshrined in the second, "personal property" map, as opposed to the "nature" map in which land had been free for use. To find my way, I had to use the two maps and was often lost.

Collecting the economic information I wanted took months. Finding a person, establishing a connection, telling her what I was doing, and asking the questions could take days. Appointments were made and not kept, and it was done in the heat of the day that affected me more than them. Reaching the selected houses required walking through savannah grass where snakes lurked. The people treated every snake as poisonous and carried machetes for protection but I was loaded with a clipboard, notebook, questionnaire, and camera, and I had little skill at killing a snake with a machete. I did not encounter snakes on these trudges in my high boots, but unknown bugs in the grass took their toll on my legs. Afterward, I resolved never to do a survey again, but the information was valuable.

***

Animals seemed to be attracted to me even when I was not in the fields. On awakening I checked my boots for scorpions before putting them on. I never found one awaiting a foot, but one morning after breakfast, I spotted a long green snake slithering in our wooden rafters. We left and went to a neighbor who was home. He disposed of it with his machete. After this experience I searched the rafters when arising or entering the house.

Seated at my table typing notes one afternoon, a nest of baby rats fell into my typewriter from above. The rats and I made quick exits. Another day a troop of army ants marched through our house from the front entrance, shielded by a hanging bug screen, to the back that was shielded as well. They paraded, and Roxane and I waited. A different encounter with bugs was more serious. As I was typing one day, a bunch of unseen critters under my feet bit my legs, which began to swell. Their feeding sent me to a doctor.

Humans inflicted a more serious malady. Every year a government team came to each house in the nation spraying for mosquitoes. When the Panama Canal was being built, American doctors had successfully fought yellow fever, malaria, and other scourges, and spraying was now practiced throughout the nation. We had been away from the village for a day and returned to find our belongings outside the house. Both it and our possessions had been sprayed with DDT that left white blotches on everything.

Within hours I had a severe allergic response. Sweaty, dizzy, and nauseous, I knew I had not been bitten and have no allergies, so it took time to realize what happened. As Roxane and I talked, I became woozier, so we left for the provincial capital.

In town, we found the sole doctor, a Chinese man. Taking me into his back room that had a few chemicals on shelves emitting an unknown odor, he had me lower my pants and lie face down on a wooden table. Turning my head, I watched as he took out a giant glass tube and plunger that seemed fit for a horse. He looked around for a time, found a bottle, filled the tube with a yellow liquid that looked like horse urine, and injected me in the butt. I trembled and shook violently for several minutes. When I stopped trembling, he said, "done." I got up feeling better but dazed and worried about what I was now carrying in my body. I did not ask.

Occasionally we went to Panama City where we would spend the first day lying in bed reading mysteries. Once I read three in a day. I used these breaks to attend to errands, and to get distance from the village, review my notes, think about what I was seeing, locate gaps and questions, and see the AID people.

Usually, we paid a visit to the Canal Zone where we could send letters from a US post office. US police cars patrolled the well-tended concrete roads in the Zone, the signs were in English, and the stores, open only to US canal personnel, carried American goods. We were allowed to eat in the cafeteria that served American food and usually selected hamburgers and mashed potatoes. Looking around, hearing only English, tasting the food, and seeing the dress and manners of the people, we thought we were in the Midwest of the United States, although we were actually visiting a five-mile-wide corridor within Panama that ran from one ocean to the other, and that housed the Canal and the US military base for the South Pacific. US citizens filled the major civilian jobs and lived in the Zone.

I was surprised that all food supplies for the Canal Zone were brought from the United States, because the Zone was directly next to Panama City. Once I visited a Zonian (US citizen), who claimed to know about peasant life, although few Zone residents spoke Spanish. She offered me a beer imported from the United States despite the tasty, less expensive Panama brands readily available forty paces across the street from her house. The woman's information about peasant life equaled her interest in drinking Panamanian beer.

The divide between the two countries and their ways of life was never more palpable than the time I drove to Panama City with Bishop McGrath. He had wanted me to go with him so I could return his car to Veraguas when he left for Rome, and I needed to report to AID. A few days before our departure I found myself plagued with a genital fungus. I had a foot fungicide and applied it liberally only to discover the difference between the two medicines. The burning was so painful I thought I would be scarred and probably impotent for life. I went with the bishop and sat in the back of the car with my pants down to cool the burning while keeping up an innocent chat with him.

We drove to the Canal Zone for a meeting the bishop would have with the US governor. The governor was a military appointee whose large house sat on the highest hill in the Zone. Built in the early twentieth century, his dwelling looked like a British colonial residence. Several stories high and constructed of wood, it was surrounded by a screen porch on the ground level. We parked and the bishop entered. I was invited to wait on the porch where I sat respectfully covered on an old-fashioned, cushioned wicker chair. A black man in a spotless white coat appeared and speaking American English asked if I would like a gin and tonic.

"I would," I said.

He brought the drink. It tasted good and I had a second. Sitting in the cool surroundings, I thought about the gulf between the two cultures, colonization, and economic power. The US enclave lasted until 1979 when the Canal was turned over to Panama.

***

Almost from our first days in the village, Roxane and I heard about religious celebrations taking place in towns throughout the central provinces. I gathered information about these celebrations as well as local rituals and beliefs, especially as the villagers had their version of Catholicism with some strange and compelling ideas and practices. The village was in the process of building a small one-room chapel under the influence of Bishop McGrath who was bringing a few priests from the United States to serve in the central provinces of Panama. In the last months of our stay a priest visited the village once, which was the first time a cleric had stopped there.

Everyone said they believed in God, but I saw a gap between the church and people in their practices and beliefs. Couples who united without civil or religious sanction were joined, as the villagers said with a sense of humor, by the "bush father." When watching mass, we saw unmarried women hanging back, for cohabiting in sin without confessing, they told us, prohibited them from taking communion.

If the uplifting side of the religion promised little to the people in the village, its chastising side was on their minds. Parents baptized their children because, they explained, it thwarted the Devil's influence (which they also did by attaching a red bracelet about a newborn's ankle and opposite wrist) and brought God into their lives through the ties of godparenthood. Their sometimes-wry view of the church was caught by the question they often posed, "How do priests remain celibate?" Stories about priests with children on the side usually followed.

The campesinos practiced one religious custom with a bit of belief, a bit more of cynicism, and a large degree of greed. Before our arrival, a group of Dutch fathers had persuaded villages around the provincial capital to purchase and circulate a small idol of the Virgin that was a replica of the one in the Santiago church. The people called it "the traveler." Each day they passed the idol from one house to another where it remained overnight so the inhabitants could pray to it. The idol sat on a donation box, and the hosting house was supposed to offer money in hope of their prayers being answered. The cash would flow to the church, but everyone told me that when the idol came to their house, they shook the box and found it empty. Others were taking what they wanted, so they did not donate.

Once a year, on 8 December, the Day of the Immaculate Conception, villages reasonably close to Santiago brought their idols to the provincial church where the main idol had a niche and a celebration was held. Savvy anthropologists might interpret the custom as a revival ceremony creating closeness to the church and fellow feeling among the populace. For the participating campesinos, it was a diversion.

No one questioned the central theology of the church, although the people had but a sketchy knowledge of it. If the sacraments bind belief to ritual, the practice side of the duality was more prominent for the people. They explained that baptism was important for securing godparents and for keeping the devil from affecting a newborn's life.

After baptism in Santiago, the religious rituals were tenuous. The Eucharist, the sacramental transmutation of bread and wine into Christ's body and blood, is a remembrance and reenactment of Christ's sacrifice, but I learned nothing of the sort in the countryside. I heard rather about the *manda* or vow, which was the principal connection formed between the people's lives in the everyday world and the church figures they deemed important, which were the saints. Central figures, such as Jesus, Mary, and Joseph, were considered to be important saints.

Making and fulfilling a *manda*, known as a *promesa* in other parts of Latin America, was the most frequent religious practice about which I heard and saw. To formulate a *manda*, a person privately appeals to a saint for help to ameliorate an earthly malady. A child or an adult might have a lasting illness or affliction, such as an injured or lame leg or a cancerous growth. Crops could be hit with a plague or lack of rain. An animal might be sick and did not respond to local remedies. The petitioner or offeror of a *manda*, who need not be the afflicted one, appeals to a saint for help and promises to donate money or perform a hardship, such as wearing a dark blue robe or walking on the knees in the procession on the saint's day, but only if the plea has been granted. The saint does not have the power to grant the request but can bring it to God who may respond. An answered request is repaid with the promised hardship. As an older woman explained: "Saints can intercede with God to help you, but you have to wait for the plea to be answered before paying the vow. You cannot coerce the saint. Saints cannot be bought." She added that if the saint does not bring the desired result, "You can try a different saint, but you can't play the saints one after another." At times, a person found a particular saint to be helpful and would bring pleas to him, but in the often-repeated phrase, "If God doesn't want it, your saint can't do it."

Almost every week I heard about one or another villager offering a *manda*, and I clutched at opportunities to understand the practice. Once a year in the small town of Atalaya, some distance away by a long road, a large celebration for "Padre Jesus" is held, and I attended several times. Outside the church, stalls have religious tokens for sale. Inside and outside the church, priests hold mass and take confession, but most of the activity revolves around paying *mandas*. I watched as people in habits, alone or with a crutch, walk the dirt road to the town, some from Panama City over 150 miles away. Spending time mingling and asking people why they were there, I found again and again that they were fulfilling a *manda*, but my attempts to discover a deeper theology or explanation of the ritual came to naught.

Eventually I viewed the *manda* as a transform or pale copy of the resurrection and the Eucharist in which earthly bread and wine miraculously become the soothing body and blood of Christ. In the successful *manda* an earthly pain, as in the resurrection, is miraculously transformed by divine power. The *manda* is an attempt to bring this power through a saintly mediator to an earthly event, shifting it from mundane control by a promised sacrifice.

On the reverse and dark side, I was told several times about a man in a neighboring village who made a pact with the devil in exchange for riches gained in animals. His Faustian trade worked until his female partner made off with his cattle, which was the typical end of those deals.

Most of the houses in the village possessed a small paper almanac that listed the saints associated with each day of the year. The almanacs were used to pick the name for a newborn in accord with the saint affiliated with its birthdate. When a different saint's name was chosen, the person might keep that saint's day, which usually meant resting instead of observing his birthday saint. The almanacs also helped people track saints' celebrations in villages and towns that were announced on the radio, and so were a *manda* reminder as well.

I was intrigued by the *manda*, because these vows to saints for everyday help stretched my credulity, far more than what I was learning about family customs and the economy, yet the *manda* seemed to be the main link between the people and the church. Bishop McGrath, who briefly discussed the practice with me and seemed to know I was not of the faith, said it was only a way to bring the people toward the church. Then, he generously gave me an embossed, four-volume work describing the lives of the saints, but my incredulity kept me going to celebrations for one or another saint in the interior provinces of the country.

Deaths and funerals fell completely outside the tendrils of the formal church. At a death, a wooden coffin is immediately purchased or hammered together. The deceased is placed in the coffin without preservation or dressing the body in special clothes. By next light a small procession carries the coffin to the local cemetery for burial with prayers offered at the grave.

Over the next eight nights a wake is held at the deceased's house. A local prayer is hired for a small sum, comes to the house and periodically utters devotions so mumbled that most of us attending could not catch his words. On these successive nights, the dead person's spirit flies around the house as in the middle period of a classic rite of passage, and the prayers help the soul of the deceased enter heaven. I attended eight wakes, some for several nights in a row. They were devoid of much talk, but attending men quietly passed bottles of the locally brewed sugarcane alcohol that people brought.

The poignant moment of the wake occurs on the final night during which some people stay praying until dawn. When the sun rises, they leave the deceased's house carrying lighted candles, crying and wailing. Outside the door, they blow out the candles, and at that moment the soul flies away. Men reshape the house so that the space where the deceased had been sleeping lies outside the bedroom walls, for the dead person's "air" is no longer in the house just as the deceased is no longer a member of the group. Both body and soul have departed.

The saddest wake we attended was for a young man, Victor, who had a partner named Carla and two young daughters. Only in his thirties, he was a drinker and inconstant worker but cheerful and friendly. Carla came from a distant village in the mountains, while Victor had family in the village. One day, after a fiesta, he was found lying by the side of a path. Carlos told me, "I came across him and gave him a kick. I looked again. Then, I went to Carla and said, 'I bring bad news.'"

Victor's wake was well attended, but its final night was difficult to watch. After the mourners had left the house, blown out the candles and reshaped the house, Victor's uncles disclaimed any responsibility for his partner and young children. They suggested that she sell the house and few belongings she had, and return to her natal village far away in the mountains where she might still have family. The widow looked bewildered, as she had made a life with her children in the village. There was silence at the uncles' abrupt severing of ties and obligation to help. The widow and her children stayed, and Roxane and I offered her occasional cash employment.

When asked about my religion, I was evasive. At Easter, flamboyant processions are held in towns and capitals. Hearing about them, I went to the province capital, Santiago, on Good Friday. A man dressed as Christ in tattered cloth and burdened with a large cross slowly advanced on the one paved street toward the provincial church. He was surrounded by Roman Centurions who were mounted on horses and urging him onward with whips they snapped in the air. Other participants on foot and still others impersonating Jews tormented this Christ with switches, while the onlooking crowd jeered the Jews as he passed. Standing to one side and watching quietly, I thought it had been wise to keep my religion private.

When I mentioned to Bishop McGrath that I had drafted some information about the local practices of godparenthood, he asked to see it, and I looked forward to his comments. Instead, he circulated my early sketch to local priests so they could know their parishioners better. I was amused that a Jew's account was informing Catholic priests about their flock and dismayed at this unintentional "applied anthropology."

***

The villagers told stories and observed certain practices that seemed penumbral to Catholicism but left me amused and puzzled about their origin. Over time, I collected five beliefs with their associated admonitions that seemed to echo the Garden of Eden story.

- If a snake bites a person, he may never touch or pick fruit from a fruit tree. If the person plucks a fruit, the tree dries up and dies, and the bitten person is contaminated for life.
- If a man has had sexual relations with a woman and in the next twenty-four hours picks fruit from a fruit tree, the tree dies. After twenty-four hours, he may take fruit without damaging the tree.
- If a pregnant woman or her partner picks fruit from a fruit tree, the tree dies. (A few times I heard a man with a ripe mango tree outside his house caution another, "Pick it with care.")

- If a pregnant woman looks at a snake, it stops moving until she takes her eyes away. This capacity is termed "The power of sight."
- If the partner of a pregnant woman kills a snake and looks at its twisting body, her baby twists and turns at birth.

When I asked for explanations of these warnings, I heard only their restatement. I asked question after question about material life and the family and achieved some understanding of these practices and beliefs, but the religious domain, consisting of practices loosely tethered to beliefs, seemed impervious to explication. Was I encountering the way Catholicism had been taught to a partly literate people over the years, was it due to the Church's inattention to the people's souls, or was my fieldwork technique at fault?

The margins of the formal beliefs, at least, fed me. Miguel told me two "true" stories about the time God was present on earth.

> One day God and the devil were walking on earth together. To taunt God, the devil secretly locked a group of men in a room and asked God to guess who was inside since he was all-powerful. God responded that the room was full of pigs. The devil laughed, opened the door, and pigs came out! For this reason, Jews, the devil's helpers, do not eat pork. Everyone was a Jew in those times.

On two other days, God was walking on earth with Saint Peter.

> On their first day a married couple had decided to have sexual relations. They were in an open area and decided to do it there. When God and Saint Peter came upon them, God turned them into a mare and stallion because, as he explained to Saint Peter, the people were acting like animals.
>
> The next day God and Saint Peter again were walking on earth. This time, hidden in the bushes, an unmarried couple was copulating. Saint Peter saw them and pointed the couple out to God. To his surprise, God let them be. When Saint Peter asked why they were not turned into horses, God explained that although the couple was not married, they were respecting others by hiding.

Whether the story reflects the power of God, Saint Peter's questioning of his power, male resistance to marrying in the church, or the importance of being circumspect sexually as in the closed bedroom of the house seemed ambiguous but that made the story ever-tantalizing, and such tales combining salacious behavior, miraculous beings, and everyday life were popular. Roxane recorded many folk tales, I wrote down others, and almost all were a mixture of humor and morality.

An oft-told narrative about a woman, the Tulivieja, seemed to be a morality tale for women. The story slightly changed with the narrator, but in one version,

> The Tulivieja was a woman who killed her child by drowning it in a brook near our village. She repented her action, but God did not forgive her. Ever since she has wandered near water with her feet turned backwards crying out for her child, and some people claim to have heard her tearful wailing. The Tulivieja can molest people, grab, or kill them. At night when people hear loud noises near the brook, they know it is the Tulivieja, but when they look the next day, they find termites.

Variations of the tale are encountered elsewhere in Panama but all the versions include themes of maternal abandonment, twisted feet, running water, and perpetual cries for a child. Ostensibly the story concerns a mother's responsibility, but I sometimes wonder if it is a tale about male power and paternal obligations. When men said they have the right to approach any female, they often justified their claim by adding, "Who knows what a woman will do? She has to defend herself." The Tulivieja story places parental responsibility on women. I heard nothing comparable for men.

I listened to these folk stories with detachment and pleasure, but when the accounts turned to witches, sorcerers, and their powers that presented an alluring world, I wished I believed them.

Witches are females who fly, appear, disappear, and sometimes bring food to someone. Roxane, who heard witch stories from women, viewed them as female fantasies of escape by flying away, just as they sometimes flee an abusive companion. The male accounts of witches fit the flighty part but with a sexual twist. One day in July 1967, Miguel told me about his encounter with a witch, which is why he believed in them.

> Miguel was in a nearby community working with his brother with whom he was staying. One night they went to bed in the dark. Miguel smoked a cigarette while lying in his bed one side of which faced the open door. On finishing his cigarette Miguel threw it on the ground near the door with his hand outstretched. Almost immediately before Miguel fell asleep, he felt something in his hand. It was a soft hand. He began to squeeze it and the hand squeezed his. "It was like shaking a hand the way she gripped." He began pulling the hand toward himself with the intention of bringing it to his chest and then giving it a big push to knock it away. He pulled hard and as he started to push, the arm went soft and his hand went between a woman's breasts. She

> came forward and rubbed her face all over his. Unable to move or speak while she was on top of him, he wanted to call for help from his brother but could only make rasping sounds. The moment the woman left, he jumped up, lit the lamp, and saw nothing.

Miguel assured me his experience was neither a dream nor a nightmare, which he has had. He was awake and had just gone to bed. The woman was a witch. Other men provided equally wondrous stories.

> A man from a nearby town, who raised bulls, was riding about on his horse one night. Suddenly the horse stopped and would go no further. The man dismounted and saw a woman's body stretched across the road and covered by a sheet. The man took a cross from his pocket and stuck it in the ground near the feet of the woman. He took a rope (like the ones that priests wear) and tied the feet of her body to the cross. He put a machete at the woman's head, so her body could not move. In the morning, the woman sat up and asked to be set free. He would not let her go until she told him where she was from and paid him not to tell her family. As she was nude, he gave her some clothing and took her on his horse to her village some distance away. She was a witch.

This magical world, alive with the power of God and women, was also home to human sorcerers. One day when I turned our topic to spells, Carlos said, "I don't know this well, but to attract a woman you get a shoe from her left foot, take it away on a Friday or Tuesday, and bury it at the foot of your door uttering a prayer. Three or four days later she gets a craze and jumps for your house where her shoe is buried. It can also be done with a hat."

He added that romantic spells can be put on a gift. The moment the woman opens the gift she leaves her house and comes to you. If offering a gift is too overt, an herbalist's powder can be bought and sprinkled on a handkerchief. When the handkerchief is shaken in front of a female, she smells it and comes to you. "Spells and potions," Carlos continued, "always work."

A woman can be attracted in other ways. "You take a clean handkerchief to the field where you are working," he recounted. "When you sweat, wipe the sweat from your armpits and crotch onto the handkerchief and squeeze it so the liquid falls into a flask. Bury the flask at a crossroads. A month later return to the spot and dig up the flask. Stick the solution into something the woman will drink, and she will want you."

Potions can make a couple split apart, Miguel explained. "First, you must get hairs from each of them. Twist the hairs together and heat them over a fire without burning them, and crush the hairs into a powder. Make a coffee and pour the crushed hairs into the coffee. Then the person who drinks the coffee will want to leave her partner." Only someone other than the couple can do it, sometimes to get the woman for himself.

Miguel then gave me a long account about helping his sister leave her partner, although he failed due to an accident. His sister was fighting with her companion, so Miguel asked the female partner of the man's brother to get the man's urine. She told her companion that she needed his brother's urine to ward off the evil eye. Miguel took the urine to a sorcerer in Santiago who looked at it and saw something bad. Following the sorcerer's instructions, he bought a jar of ointment, made a hole in it and gathered water from several rivers where a black pig was resting and eating. Miguel poured the water into the hole in the ointment and covered the jar. When the mixture is ready and secretly applied to someone, he becomes angry with his partner and leaves. For the potion to work only a third person, such as Miguel, can purchase the ointment, add the water, and provide the potion.

Miguel should have given the potion to his sister so she could secretly apply it to her partner. Unfortunately, he bought the ointment on Good Friday, had a few drinks, and fell asleep at home. On awaking he removed the jar from his pocket but it hit a chair and broke. He did not try again because it would have been difficult to get more urine surreptitiously.

Roxane and I knew one instance when sorcery worked. After Eugenia left Jacinto and did not return from Panama City, he went to a distant town for help from a well-known sorcerer who uttered secret spells that made Eugenia cry no matter that she was in the capital 150 miles away. She returned. The magic worked.

I was sad to leave this wondrous world, but after eighteen months the fieldwork came to an end. I had gaps in the material but was reasonably confident about what I did know, although I did not know what I did not know. But what I did not know pointed as much to what I did not know about myself as to what I did not know about the people and their life, and this lack of self-reflection hindered my understanding of the Panamanians. I had watched and listened to them, taken notes, and followed up dangling threads. I could make my way around their life without committing too many errors. I could describe how they made a living and lived together and sometimes disagreed one with another. I had tasted what they tasted and could compare and contrast their way of living with ours. My fieldwork was down-to-earth but so was my thinking about their life including their rituals. I saw their rituals as add-ons, as flourishes, and sometimes as costs, to be recorded and interpreted as in the case of godparenthood. I did not realize for many years that much of their life might be seen as a kind of ritual including their ways of practicing and thinking about agriculture, organizing work parties, and arranging family life. And if that were so, then the same word, ritual, also might be used for our own apparently grounded, rationally calculated, money mediated, material ways of sustaining our life through which I was understanding their ways of sustaining life. I did not realize that even the anthropologist's word "culture," often used as the cover term for the practices and beliefs of a people, might be replaced by the word "ritual." As the journey proceeded in other places, I gathered more illustrations of this ritual way of viewing a people's life, but it remained too far from my matter-of-fact beginnings for me to arrive at that realization until late in the journey, so I used the word "culture" for the different ways of conducting life that I observed.

***

Returning to England in autumn 1967, I began work on the PhD dissertation based on the research. The next year and a half was filled with blind alleys. I had the uncategorized daily notes, the focused interviews, material in my head, a census of the village, kinship charts, and the economics questionnaire. I wanted to develop the theme about godparenthood in relation to the family and the house but moving from insight to argument was a daunting task.

Since that time, I have come to relish analysis, which is the pleasure of research, but that was not my feeling then. I experienced cognitive dissonance again as I had no models to follow, and nothing fit together. I reviewed the field materials, jotted down notes on scraps of paper that I could not decipher, shuffled and reshuffled information in my head with hopes a plan would emerge. I wrote brief sections but found they did not fit other scribbles or were irrelevant. The magic of the field was replaced by the drudgery of sitting at a desk.

These months had moments of diversion. One day Roxane and I traveled to a village outside Cambridge where professional weavers used looms that were a century old. Each bolt of cloth had a distinctive design that required different threads to be woven in a specific way. I was fascinated to see that the order of the shuttles for a loom was coded on a continuous metal chain with holes that turned the sprockets, which ran the shuttles in the design's order. The design was set in the chain, and the weavers each had a rack of different chains, which could be used to produce different textile designs. I suddenly realized that the coding system for my day notes on the yellow cards with their potential holes around the edges that could be punched out to encode different topics and combinations was a descendent of this weaving system, which itself was an ancestor of modern computing. The weavers were successful in their task. I was not.

I needed to find a job, especially now that our first daughter, Rebecca, had been born in 1968. Far removed from the job scene in the United States and knowing little about how it operated, I contacted Evon Vogt, who told me about several openings, and I chose Minnesota for its department, the state's political climate, and because Roxane could transfer to Minnesota's Institute of Child Development where she could use her data to complete a PhD. We moved to Minneapolis in the summer of 1969 where Elise was born in 1970 and Keren in 1975.

I began shaping the godparenthood material into an essay and started reading canon law and its history beginning with John's baptism of Christ and the subsequent elaborations. Turning eventually to St. Thomas Aquinas' *Summa Theologica*, written in the thirteenth century, I was delighted to find that he not only developed the logic of reasoning by analogy, which is central to structuralism, but applied it to godparenthood. Aquinas used the four-part analogy that natural parents are to spiritual parents as birth is to rebirth. His analogical argument had a major impact on the later Council of Trent (1545–63) that set forth the ideological form and church regulations for godparenthood that were transmitted to the New World. What I had found in a far-removed zone of the church fit the central ideas and canon law changes that evolved over two millennia and was substantially conceptualized by Aquinas.

One afternoon after teaching several classes I was trying to put my material together, hit a dead end, and decided to go home. As I was driving, the final piece occurred to me. I pulled into the nearest parking lot, which happened to be a nun's residence, found a scrap of paper, and made a note. The child in the earthly family is given away to be reborn at baptism by godparents who are in other houses. This giving of the child establishes him as a natural person within his natal home and a spiritual person in the godparent's house, and so links the two through co-parenthood. With this ideological framework I had a structuralist analysis of godparenthood, an exchange analysis based on sharing the personhood of the child, a functional analysis showing how the *compadrazgo* was used in Panama, a cultural analysis based on church ideology and ritual, a historical recounting of church laws showing its many variations as the ideology was refined over the centuries, and a comparative analysis that included every ethnographic study I could find all of which fit the underlying pattern (Gudeman 1972).

***

By this time General Omar Torrijos had led a coup and taken over the Panamanian government. Born and educated in Santiago, Veraguas, Torrijos was a populist and authoritarian leader, who was especially sympathetic to the campesinos. His government adopted the *Veraguas Report* that I wrote with George Lodge and the *Plan de Veraguas* that I helped write with a group sponsored by the Bishop. Then, he built a government sugarcane mill some miles from the village where we had lived. Lodge told me that when a Goldman Sachs representative visited Torrijos, who was seeking external financing, Torrijos pulled out the two reports from his desk drawer and called them "My bible."

The government also took over a very large piece of land that included the village where we had lived as well as neighboring ones and converted the entire area to growing sugarcane, except for strips left for houses. The entire enterprise was organized as a cooperative, following our approach, and some of the local cooperative leaders I knew became administrators, although military officers soon replaced them.

I had to see what happened and returned to the village in the early 1970s. The entire land area was now divided into large plots, with aerial spraying and other modern methods used to raise the sugarcane. The old paths, landmarks, and subsistence crops had disappeared, as had the individual plots. The people's mental maps were useless now, but the larger plots of sugarcane were numbered with metal signs for orientation. All the houses in the village, once scattered in savannah grass, shrub, and woods, were grouped along freshly cut mud roads. Male villagers were guaranteed work in the mill's fields and were transported there by truck every day, but dissidents were dismissed including my friend, Miguel, who fled to the Darien jungle on the border with Colombia.

The people still ate rice at every meal but now they bought it in hundred-pound sacks with their wages and cooked it on propane stoves, for the sources of wood had disappeared. Many houses were now made of bricks, supplemented by the stick form, and all were linked to electric lines. When I visited several homes, I heard strange voices, looked inside and saw television sets playing Latin American soap operas. The use of battery-powered radios had disappeared.

The villagers were pleased with the change as their standard of living had improved, but I was ambivalent. Much of what I had studied about economy had disappeared, but the people's material life in terms of food, clothing, and shelter was better, and it was churlish to be nostalgic. I was not concerned that the change made my research dated, because I knew it held for larger areas and for the time it was done. I was concerned by the forced turn to dependence on a single crop and by the nationalistic-militaristic tone of the government that forced the change.

As I traveled along the highway that traverses Panama, I saw military bases had been built for use if liberation from a hostile uprising was needed and as signs of control. Billboards along the road promoted nationalistic themes with Torrijos' pictures and mottos that had a religious flavor. One read, "The only thing I have against Christ is that he died without fighting." Another posting stated, "On our feet or dead but never on our knees." Both calls to action were directed against US control of the Canal. I could not decide if I preferred these billboards to my previous favorite that read "You have a friend at the Chase Manhattan," because no one in the countryside had a bank account at the Chase, and I could never figure out to whom that billboard was directed. These postings and similar radio announcements directed against the United States did not influence my relations with the villagers who never mentioned them.

When I met with one of the priests at the bishopric in Santiago, he motioned me to follow him outside the bishop's residence to an open sided rancho in back. I was puzzled, because the residence was new and cool inside. After we were seated, he put his finger to his lips and said, "Sapos" (literally toads, but also meaning informers). Then, he told me about oppression against dissidents. Because the church was helping campesinos in the countryside, socially active priests were coming under scrutiny. I leaned forward as he continued in a lowered voice telling me about a happening in the bishopric. In a nearby mountain village (that he named) a priest, who backed the campesinos against encroaching landowners, suddenly disappeared. Men in a military helicopter picked him up and dropped him in the Atlantic Ocean.

After my visits, village optimism about the possibilities brought by the new mill plunged, for the world price of sugar fell with immediate and adverse effects on the campesinos.

I never found out the degree to which my roundabout communications to Torrijos contributed to the changes in the village, but they and my earlier encounter with a columnist during fieldwork were not the only unintended outcomes of the Panama work. Before I went to Panama for the initial fieldwork, I obtained a copy of the US Army's *Warfare Area Handbook for Panama*. Intended to be useful for an invading army, it contained background material about the country including information about the countryside, such as the weather, local economy and the people's living arrangements. After I published articles and a book based on the fieldwork, I again purchased the handbook but found it had been relabeled *Area Handbook for Panama*. The new handbook drew on my published material and included expanded information about social life, beliefs, economy, and the political situation in the countryside. I shuddered that it might be used for military purposes.

In late 1989, the United States invaded Panama to capture General Manuel Noriega, who had succeeded General Torrijos, after his airplane mysteriously crashed. The US invasion focused on the area near the Canal, but the US military also used an older airstrip about an hour from where we had lived to land soldiers. One rumor suggested that Noriega had hidden deep in the Panama countryside, presumably in the Veraguas area where we had been located. Noriega was eventually found hiding in the residence of the Papal Nuncio in Panama City. United States forces that were directed by General Colin Powell, who became Chairman of the Joint Chiefs of Staff and then as Secretary of State supported the first Iraq war, flushed him out. My field studies would have been useless in the search for Noriega or for invading the countryside, but I took notice of their use by the US government.

***

My trip to Panama in 1974 ended in sadness. In addition to the village visit, I wanted to know more about the remaining Guaymi people who were descendants of the original inhabitants. The Guaymi were located in the northern part of Veraguas in the rain forest across the mountainous continental divide. Was their economy, social form, and house life comparable to that of the campesinos? Both lived in a broadly similar environment. Could I find cultural connections between the two that would enlighten my earlier work or had history either prevented or eradicated any connection? Reputedly, the Guaymi practiced cross-cousin marriage.

In 1949, Claude Lévi-Strauss published a pathbreaking book about cousin marriage. It galvanized the profession and was a precursor to his later development of structuralism. Cross-cousins are offspring of a brother and sister. Parallel cousins are offspring of same sex siblings. Lévi-

Strauss showed how marriage between cross-cousins in many parts of the world links together lineages or families whereas marriage between parallel cousins does not. The first creates social solidarity, while the second does not and seems to be rare, but finding Lévi-Strauss's model in the field requires collecting and analyzing a people's kinship terminology, as well as their lineage and marriage arrangements. By the 1970s, innumerable publications had emerged confirming, expanding, and criticizing his theory. I wanted to find out if the godparenthood system fit with or perhaps had replaced cross-cousin marriage, because the two might perform broadly similar roles in social life and because my analysis of godparenthood had been influenced by Lévi-Strauss' theory.

While I was in Los Boquerones, I met two campesinos who lived near the Guaymi and were returning to their homes in the mountains. We arranged that I would drive us to a small village in the mountains below the continental divide. From there we would climb, cross the divide and descend by foot through the dense rainforest that covered the area. I knew that Columbus had landed on the north coast of the province and given the name *Veragua* (to see water) to the area. He heard there was gold in the region but was defeated by the jungle in his vain search for treasure.

After driving upward for hours on a one-lane mud road in an old four-wheel drive Land Rover that I borrowed from a friend in Panama City, my companions and I set out from a highland village where I left the vehicle. I had a new backpack and carried a load of food for myself and for the people I would visit. My two companions, who were in their thirties and energetic, happily returned to the rain forest, but I struggled weighed down by my pack, heat, and lack of jungle experience. I was in my thirties and though my conditioning was decent, I grew weary in the muggy climate, my glasses steamed over, and I could not see very far. My companions drank from streams, but I was cautious. At times they cut a path through the dense foliage.

To cross the continental divide, we climbed to 5,000 feet, although the conditions made it feel higher. After three hours a shoulder strap on my backpack broke. The others, who had burlap bags strapped to their backs with vines, stopped. One took out his machete, cut a vine, and fashioned it into a strap, although he paused briefly to kill a poisonous snake I had not seen. Finally, we crossed the divide, descended for several hours, and in the evening reached a collection of stick houses where we were offered a soup of root crops and stayed for the night in a hut.

Our enclosed shelter was on a raised platform made of thin logs on which we slept with about ten other men. I listened to snores, farts, and other noises into the night until I finally had to pee. I did what they did which was to stand in the doorway and pee from the door rather than descend the notched pole. In the morning I understood the practice, because when I climbed down, I found at the bottom one of the well-known snakes, known as an equis (fer-de-lance) whose bite reputedly permitted a person to walk three steps before falling over dead. I thought it was dead and gave it a kick, and found it was. One of the men said a chicken must have bitten it, while I wondered about my sanity after kicking it.

I talked with some people in the village and listened to a five-hour meeting about building a school, however we had not reached the Guaymi, who were further down the mountain in the jungle, and my guides now decided to stop. To go farther would require a day or more, and no one was available to guide me. Some of the people told me about two missionaries who had a place among the Guaymi and that I might be able to reach the group through these missionaries.

The following day, after trudging back up the mountain with other companions as guides, I reached the car in late afternoon and descended to Santiago where I drank an enormous quantity of water. The next day I was driving back to Panama City to resume the quest by air, when the borrowed Land Rover gave out as I reached the city's edge. The road was downhill, and I coasted to an old hotel where I left the car. I called my friend who had lent it. She said it was worthless, and I should abandon it on the street.

The following day I found that the missionaries were a pair of evangelicals from the Summer Institute of Linguistics that had other teams in Panama. All were US citizens. Their task in Panama as elsewhere was to live among a native group, learn the language, translate the Bible for the people's edification, and foster their salvation. As one wag in Spanish said about the group, "neither summer, nor institute, nor linguistics." I decided to suppress my reservations about their project if that was the only way to reach the Guaymi. I also was interested to see what the evangelicals did.

At the head office of the Summer Institute of Linguistics in Panama City, I learned that the group had a small airplane, which flew weekly supplies to each of its teams scattered in remote parts of the country. After some discussion, they agreed that I could go on the flight to the north coast of Veraguas and stay with the missionary pair for a short time. Pleased at their acceptance of an anthropologist, I arranged to meet the American pilot the next day at a small airport outside Panama City.

He arrived in old jeans and a faded gray shirt and told me we needed to get fuel for the plane, which I thought might have been obtained at the airport, but we climbed into his car with some gas cans. I did not mind the delay, except he spent the trip telling me about Christ and his personal moment of illumination, while asking for my views about God and trying to convert me. "You will feel free. You will be a better person. Your cares will fall away," he said and added, "You need to find Christ in your life. What do you think?"

Given my still unrepentant feelings about ritual, I stalled because I wanted the plane ride and said again and again in response to his probing, "I don't know, I don't know."

Finally, I brought closure with what I hoped was a suggestive mutter, "We'll see, we'll see."

On returning to the airport, I saw that the plane had a single propeller, was old and small, and had a narrow space for cargo behind its two seats. I started to get in when the pilot told me to go to the front of the plane. From his seat, he yelled, "contact," which I figured meant start the propeller. I yanked it down, stood back, saw a puff of smoke when the engine started, and climbed in. The front of the airplane had a thick steel muzzle, like a dog's. Slightly alarmed, I asked what it was for, and he said, "You never know when you are going to crash in the jungle." He added that he never worried because God would protect him, and he began to pray. I was concerned by his explanation and not calmed by his prayer but hoped it covered both of us.

The ride, a few hundred feet above ground, was bumpy. We went west along the country, then toward the mountains and over the divide, and finally downward slightly above the rain forest. After a time, I saw in the distance a slight cutting in the trees. Descending to the narrow area cleared of growth, we landed going uphill, stopping just short of more forest. The husband of the two evangelicals met me, and we carried the supplies to their hut while the airplane took off.

Their wooden hut sat on stilts. In the doorway above us stood the young wife, dressed in a long white dress, which seemed strange in the wet, muddy surroundings. They invited me to share meals with them and showed me a nearby, dilapidated hut also on stilts where I could lay my sleeping bag on its plank floor.

The couple's hut had a second room where the husband worked with two Guaymi translators rendering the Wycliffe Bible into their language eventually to convert all the people. He had been employing the two for more than a year. The room also contained a shortwave, battery-operated radio as the Panama office of the Summer Institute of Linguistics kept in daily contact with its teams, partly for emergency purposes.

Over lunch the couple said they were from farms in North Dakota. They mentioned a few persons that I might find to interview, and I went for a walk in the hamlet that contained eight houses, while more were scattered in the rain forest. At dinner I told the couple what I had seen and who I had met. The wife said she had never been as far as I walked.

The husband did not leave the house when I was there, except to meet me when I arrived. Each day, he worked with his assistants, while the wife kept house. Given their air supplies, radio, fresh food flown to them, and purpose as well as lack of interest in the life of the people, the difference between their religious endeavor and my anthropological one was striking, but the husband who had a master's degree in linguistics expressed interest in studying anthropology at the University of Minnesota after he finished his translation and the Guaymi Bible was ready for converting the people.

Over the next days, I visited stick and thatch houses that looked similar to ones in the lowlands where Roxane and I had lived. Most were not on stilts. Men worked small fields that had been cleared in the rain forest, and their crops looked similar to the campesinos'. Their clothing was familiar as well, although Spanish clearly was not their first language, and men had better facility speaking it. Interviewing a few people, I found they lived in single-family houses and did not practice godparenthood, but their native kinship terminology encoded cross-cousin marriage. The beginning part of my quest was successful, but I needed to have more information about the connection between their terminology, kinship system, and actual marriages, and my time did not allow for more than a start on those topics. I would have to come back for an extended study.

On the day for my return to Panama City, I was sitting outside interviewing a man and gathering more information about Guaymi kinship terminology and marriage arrangements, when the plane appeared in the sky, signaling the end of the inquiry. The plane landed going uphill as before, but the strip was muddy from rain, and the pilot stopped short of the end in muck. I threw my backpack in and was ready for the "contact" command, prayers and takeoff, but the pilot told me that after starting the propeller, I should go to the rear and push the plane to get it going in the mud. I did, and as it was rolling downhill, ran to the side and jumped in. We gained a little speed and took off scraping the tops of the trees at the bottom of the strip. The trip back was filled with wind gusts that violently shook the plane until we touched down in Panama City.

Now began the sad end to this sally. My parents had moved to Florida about a year before because Dad had retired and was ill. After visiting him in Florida on the way to Panama from Minneapolis, I learned his cancer was getting worse. Immediately on returning to Panama City, I telephoned Roxane and learned that my parents had gone to New York where he was now in hospital. I reserved a seat for the next day's flight to New York, arrived that evening in my field clothes, and went directly to see my father. Our visit was brief, and I returned the next morning. We had a longer talk when suddenly he had a seizure, alarms sounded, and nurses and a doctor rushed into the room. I was told to leave, and he was rolled to the emergency operating theater. He never regained consciousness and died the next day. My mother said he stayed alive to see me. Nixon resigned in those days. I have not been back to Panama since.

## Notes

1. My thanks to George Lodge who in 2021 read drafts of these sections and offered corrections and suggestions. George reiterated that he was always interested in change and development as the outcome of technical and monetary aid rather than the narrower goal of "economic growth," and he has written extensively on these topics. He mentioned that he was vastly outspent in his senatorial campaign against Ted Kennedy and had a campaign debt that lingered for a decade.
2. Bishop McGrath was born in the Canal Zone to an American father of Irish descent, who had worked on building the Canal, and to a Costa Rican mother. He had become a Panamanian citizen.

CHAPTER 4

# Life and Text Together

In the early 1970s, I was vexed by the material on economy I had collected and by the question of economic development. The United States had poured more money per capita into Panama than any other nation, but this assistance was not reaching the people in the countryside. I saw that I had lived in an early seedbed of development efforts that were largely ineffective.

The Marshall Aid Plan after World War II had pumped more than 36 billion dollars (at today's prices) into the United Kingdom and other amounts into Europe. Designed to revive existing market structures and promote economic development, the plan was impelled by the motives of reviving commercial trade, opening new markets for the United States, and vaccinating against communism. US financial assistance to Panama, directed to building infrastructure for the expansion of commercial trade and protecting the Canal, had similar objectives.

Prior to fieldwork, while I was at the Business School, I had been admonished that economic development occurs only through "external shocks" (later known as "shock therapy," meaning a rapid change from state control to free markets as a cure for unemployment, inflation, and other economic maladies). The theory was advocated for Chile in 1975 and for some postsocialist countries in the 1990s with almost deleterious effects. The only shock with which Panama's countryside could be associated was the building of the government sugarcane mill, partly influenced by my work. But the mill had lethal effects on the environment and diverse livelihood of the people in the village where we lived.

During the original fieldwork, I spent time with Panamanian agronomists who, in the name of development, asked me what crops should be grown in the countryside. Technology transfer was their key to "advancing" because it would raise productivity, increase food supplies, and help local growers. I saw little evidence of these efforts or their effects in Panama. Technological transfer requires educational support, direct assistance in the field, and financial backing, which were lacking.

The business case I wrote was directed to business leaders to expand their knowledge of the countryside, broaden their outlook, and lead to greater support for rural folk. It may have been useful in Harvard's classrooms, but I have no indication that it helped the rural areas of Panama or anywhere else in Latin America.

As for the prior sugar mills in Panama, the owners and managers claimed they were developing the countryside by turning rural folk to cash cropping and offering wage labor, but this commercialization of farming came at the cost of household provisioning and environmental degradation, while allowing the mills to lower the cost of their suppliers who provided their own sustenance and avoid rental payments for use of the land. It was a form of outsourcing.

The people wanted better nutrition, better schooling for their children, better medical care, and better land. The two studies of material conditions in the countryside that I co-authored were intended to raise awareness of these local problems and promote communal organizations, but the studies led to the government enterprise that purchased the land, which the village people previously had used for free to raise their daily food. This development project, carried out under the mantra of helping the people by forming a government cooperative, completed the environmental devastation that began with the cash crop, destroyed the existing subsistence economy, and led to political and military repression by General Torrijos. My discontent with these projects kept me away from further involvement with development efforts.

***

Frustrated by the inability of business approaches and standard economics to capture what I had seen in Panama, I started to think anthropologically about the village economy and in terms of its larger context rather than as a sum of individual choices as in market economics. Roxane and I may have lived in an economic "backwater," although it was very lively, but that designation implied the existence of a "front water." How were they related?

I turned first to Latin American "structuralist economics" and "dependency theory," which focused on the relation between development in the industrialized world and underdevelopment in Latin America. The theories insisted that growth in the north was tied to stagnation and immiseration in the south. I knew the campesinos worked hard, so their "lack" of economic development could not be attributed to low motivation. The Panamanian mill owners were wealthy, the United States was receiving low-cost raw sugar ready for refining, and the campesinos were struggling as they provided the sugarcane on which the external wealth was built. My field material illustrated the general perspectives of dependency and structuralist theory; however, these theories lacked a foundation in the way local economies worked.

When I gravitated to Karl Marx and to his predecessor David Ricardo, the Panama material on economy suddenly came together for I was analyzing it in terms of labor. Using numbers from the time-consuming and irksome questionnaire and measuring everything by days of work, I saw that by shifting to the cash crop, sugarcane, the people were unable to buy with its monetary return as much rice for the house as they had previously grown on the same piece of land. The shift to cash cropping and a market economy was a losing deal, which I described in the book *The Demise of a Rural Economy*.

***

In 1976, I met Clifford Geertz who had recently joined the Institute for Advanced Study in Princeton. We talked briefly and a few weeks later he invited me to come to the Institute for the academic year 1978–1979 when a group of nontraditional economists would be in residence. The Institute was established for Albert Einstein in the 1930s when he fled Germany. We were provided a small house on Einstein Drive on the Institute's grounds. Roxane had an office in the house, Rebecca and Elise attended school in Princeton, and Keren went to the Institute's nursery school.

The Institute funds members to think and write without other duties, except to have lunch with others every day and participate in a weekly seminar in its School of Social Science. The Institute focuses primarily on theoretical physics and math, but the opening to the social sciences had begun.

At the time, the Institute was celebrating Einstein's "miraculous year" (1905) when he published four papers that changed physics, and for the celebration, a collection of Nobel Prize winners presented talks about his work. The social scientists were allowed to attend these gatherings but had to sit in the balcony. The conference focused mostly on the Theory of Special Relativity, although some speakers mentioned the

Theory of General Relativity that Einstein published a decade afterward, and from his wheelchair Stephen Hawking spoke about black holes, but Einstein's later theory did not receive extended mention.

The time lags in the incorporation of Einstein's succession of ideas led me to reflect on a difference between anthropology and the hard sciences. In the sciences, theories are superseded or destroyed by new discoveries, falsifications, and insights. In anthropology, popular ideas and theories float around, are used to justify one or another ethnographic finding, and then are replaced by another set of concepts loosely linked or tangential to what came before.

I was able to join the resident economists when they discussed their papers and brought in speakers, and learned about the cutting edges of the field. Two of the participants later received Nobel prizes. But the economists' approaches and vision of their field were closer to the hard sciences than they were to anthropology. I saw that one could talk about progress in the hard sciences and to a degree in economics, but what about anthropology? Is it closer to a science, an interpretive perspective, or a bit of both?

At this point, although I was not fully aware of the shift, my adventure bifurcated or perhaps doubly divided, and my objective became to bridge the divides. I was following a series of mental journeys that I wanted to interweave with the field journeys, and I was traveling my own unplanned trails in economics that I wished to link to anthropological perspectives. I wanted anthropological findings to be theoretically informed, and I wanted to interweave economics with anthropology in a more thorough way than had previously been done. My goals probably represented my own divide between a commonsense worldview and fascination with more ritualistic ways of formulating life.

I spent the year at the Institute trying to develop cultural economics. It would veer from standard neoclassical economics by exploring folk models or the shared ideas and practices in a people's material life rather than by deploying an externally formulated model to explain them to us, such as rational choice, competitive markets, the desire for gain and other accepted assumptions. Terming a people's designs "local models" in contrast to the universal ones of economics, I then wondered if I could reverse the perspective to see a group of economists who shared a paradigm as if they were a "tribe" and their model as culturally formulated not to speak of our own living economy?

To start, I turned to a school of early French economists, the physiocrats, who were influential in the decades before the French Revolution.

Physiocracy means "rule of nature," for these economists believed that all value comes from the land. Seed multiplies due to the land's fertility, while animals grow by drawing on nature's bounty. The actual work of farmers who sow and harvest the land, and care for animals is considered "barren." The farmers do receive a return from the land to support their work and materials but no more. The aristocrats, however, who own the productive land receive, and rightly so, everything above these expenses of farming.

Decades after their work, the physiocrats were denigrated by Marx for obscuring the place of human labor, but I was drawn to them for their difference from contemporary economics and especially because their theory loosely resembled Panamanian ideas that only nature is productive. Like the farmers depicted by the physiocrats, the campesinos see themselves as passive though necessary participants when raising crops, as in their barber image of the agriculturalist who "cuts" the "hair" growing up from the "skull" (the earth).

I realized then that the Panamanian understanding drew on metaphors—hair, skull, and clipping—and wondered if this more symbolic mode of analysis would help me grasp the physiocrats as well. Eventually I saw the physiocratic model as a combination of images drawn from John Locke's epistemology (with which they were very familiar) that distinguishes between active sensations drawn from the world and passive operations in the mind, and from the physiocrat François Quesnay's knowledge as a doctor of the circulation of blood and of birth or reproduction. These three images of the human body consisting of sensations and operations, of circulation, and of reproduction overlap when they are projected on the land and suggest that it is the source of economic value, which was the physiocratic claim. Their picture of economy was modeled after or was a metaphor of their understanding of the human body.

I was pleased with this undermining foray into Western economics but had ventured into treacherous waters. An anthropological analysis suggesting that metaphors provide the structure for an important, though now rejected, Western model of the economy did not rest well with believers in economics as a progressive science or with Marxists who see labor as the source of all value. For Marx and his followers, physiocracy was a "mystification" that hid the role of labor as the source of value.

Something different troubled me, however. The physiocrats and the Panamanians thought nature was the source of economic value, but the physiocrats claimed that land yielded a "net product" above expenditures, while the Panamanians did not think agriculture provided a profit or an extra above cost. Why was there a difference? The answer was there, but I took years to realize it.

Learning about physiocracy with its focus on land as economy's single fertile source planted a seed in my head about ecology and the second law of thermodynamics or entropy. I had witnessed land devastation in Panama after the advent of the cash crop, sugarcane, which made subsequent use of the earth for rice, maize, and other crops impossible. One anthropologist had written about ecology and economy among the Tsembaga Maring of New Guinea (Rappaport 1978), showing that when the people grew more and more pigs, they overused local resources and potentially upended their economy; however, the people periodically slaughtered the pigs for ritual feasts, which practice allowed the natural resources to regenerate and brought the ecology into balance ready for another cycle of pig inflation and their subsequent destruction. In contrast, in Panama I saw not cyclical destruction and regeneration but irreversible devastation, because the lateritic soil in Panama could not be used again and again if the forest that nourished it was destroyed unless fertilizer and other nourishing agents were added.

As I was driving back to Minnesota from the Institute, with physiocracy, land fertility, and ecology in mind, I continually stopped to read a book by the economist Nicholas Georgescu-Roegen, *The Entropy Law and the Economic Process* (1971). (Roxane and our daughters left after I did and took a scenic route while I drove a small trailer with our belongings.) At once startling and worrying, and written decades before the overuse of resources and global warming became world issues, Georgescu-Roegen argued that accepted economics had not taken account of entropy. By the first law of thermodynamics, energy is conserved or maintained in a closed system, but by the second law, it becomes less organized (and less available for human use), which is the entropic process, for the sun is our only source of new energy. I was struck by the discrepancy between the second, entropy law of thermodynamics, and our market stories that "growth is good, more growth is better." (We shortly thereafter put solar panels on the south-facing roof of our house.)

Despite my new attentiveness to the physical laws relating to use of the environment, I did not connect them to what the Panamanians told me half a decade earlier. After a day of work in the fields men would say, "I am *cansado*, (tired, weary) and will be better tomorrow but not *estropeado* (worn out, broken, damaged), for I will rest and eat." Only when I reached Colombia and learned about making, keeping, and using "the base," which is a reservoir of vital energy that is expended in daily living, did I grasp the resonance of the Panamanian's words with the first and second laws of thermodynamics.

***

In 1983–84, I was in Cambridge, England where, associated with King's and the anthropology department, I continued with a cultural analysis of economy by exploring ethnographies and economic theory. Dissatisfied with Marx's theory of labor value as a critique of capitalism and analysis of economy, I turned to Ricardo on whom Marx drew. Ricardo initially set forth a land value theory of economy, which partially harmonized with physiocracy, although he soon shifted to a theory of labor value to explain how prices work. His clarity, originality, and deductive reasoning gripped the analytical side of my mental divide, although his reliance on deductive thinking hardly fit what I witnessed in fieldwork and saw in the ethnographies I was reading.

Several interests began to overlap, however. I had long been a devotee of the work of Karl Polanyi (1944, 1968), the economic historian. He urged that land and labor are the "substance" or building blocks of all economies, and their interaction makes up society's life process. Neither land nor labor is produced for sale and so are "fictitious [or false] commodities" when brought to the market. Polanyi was critical of unregulated market society and standard market theory for "dis-embedding" economy from its social and material matrix and claiming that it obeys separate market laws.

While at Cambridge exploring words and meanings in relation to economy, I came across a striking example that in a circuitous way linked Polanyi's view of land and labor as the productive elements in society to a rather radical economist. One afternoon in the King's College library, I saw on display under glass some handwritten letters. Joan Robinson, the economist, had recently died and bequeathed them to the College. Several of them, written in the 1930s when the postal service delivered twice a day, were between her and the economist, Piero Sraffa, who was editing the Ricardo papers and developing his own destabilizing views. Some of their messages were about meeting for tea in the afternoon, but two captured my eye, because they related to ideas I was pursuing. Sraffa had set off a debate in economics about the existence of capital with a book (*Production of Commodities by Means of Commodities*) published in 1960.

The controversy revolved about the idea of capital as a "real" thing like labor and resources, which is why his words written two decades before his book was published attracted me. The librarian allowed me to copy extracts from the letters if I used pencil and paper on top of the glass display case. One section of a letter from Sraffa to Robinson sent in the early 1930s read:

> 1) I have never said "that there is no possibility of having a serious subject dealing with human beings": this I should regard as mystical bunk.
>
> 2) Also I have no doubts as to the seriousness of Economics. I think that Economics (i.e. the contents of Mcmillan's blue tomes) has taken in modern society to a large extent the place that theology had in the Middle Ages: and there has never been any thing as serious as that.
>
> 3=1+2) It is just because one thinks that theology cannot stand rational criticism that one regards as possible a scientific study of the objects of theology (e.g. the origin of man, physical cosmogony, etc.). I mean to say that the fog is not outside, in the air or in human society, but inside the heads of theogians [*sic*] (and economists). (letter dated 31 October 1932)

Sraffa penned a second letter to Robinson four years later (27 October 1936):

> If one measures labour and land by heads or acres the result has a definite meaning, subject to a margin of error: the margin is wide, but it is a question of degree. On the other hand if you measure capital in tons the result is purely and simply nonsense. How many tons is, e.g., a railway tunnel? If you are not convinced, try it on someone who has not been entirely debauched by economics. Tell your gardener that a farmer has 200 acres or employs 10 men—will he not have a pretty accurate idea of the quantities of land + labour? Now tell him that he employs 500 tons of capital, + he will think you are dotty – (not more so, however, than Sidgwick or Marshall).

I loved Sraffa's spare writing that debunked the idea of capital as a real entity. It resonated with Polanyi's that emphasized land and labor as the bedrock of economy, and I relished Sraffa's offhand comparison of some economists to theologians because it fertilized my germinating thought that economy might be rather like a ritual.

The debunking of capital by Sraffa sent me back to David Ricardo who showed how profit and rent are inversely related, which is to say the higher the rent, the lower the profit and the reverse, and that argument in turn returned me to the issue of meaning in economics and economies. According to Ricardo's first argument about rent on land and profit on capital, when tariffs on imported food increase, profits fall and rents rise (1815). Conversely, when tariffs are lowered or eliminated, profits rise and rents fall. The same plot of land would yield either more rent to the land owner and less profit to the capitalist farmer, or more profit to the capitalist farmer and less rent to the landowner depending on the size of the tariff.

The argument seemed convincing, but I was caught by a shift in the meanings that Ricardo attached to the returns from land and from capital, because according to Ricardo profit and rent have different sources. Rent, said he, is "the remuneration given to the landlord for the use of the original and inherent power of the land," (1951–52: IV:18) while profit is a return on capital, but this led to a contradiction.

When the farming frontier changes through expansion or contraction, so does the relation of rent and profit, because profit across the entire surface is competitively determined by the last and least productive plot tilled. A shift outward in the land frontier (when tariffs are raised and less productive land must be farmed) means that profit for the capitalist, which has been taken on an inside plot, is lowered due to its competition with the last and least productive plot that has to be farmed, and this profit return on land sets the rate for the entire country. In reverse, when the land frontier contracts (because tariffs are lowered, low-cost grains are imported, and less—but more productive—land is farmed), the capital return (as determined by the least but now comparatively more productive plot) rises, takes up what previously had been taken as rent for use of the land, and sets the competitive rate, which is advantageous for the country. In the one case, the landowner receives part of what previously was profit on a plot. In the other, the capitalist farmer gets part of what the landowner previously collected for a plot. The same plot farmed in the same way to grow the same thing can yield either profit on capital or rent on land, depending on how much land is farmed given the tariff. So, did this mean that profit on capital also was a return for land's "original and inherent power"?

I stopped there satisfied to show the contradictory meanings deployed in an early, deductive economic model that was a forerunner of marginalist analysis in economics. I might have arrived at a more interesting conclusion. Years later, after economists expanded the idea of "rent" to include any unearned return secured beyond labor's recompense, my analysis of Ricardo's shifting line between the capitalist's profit and the landowner's rent made sense. Like interest received for a loan or royalties received for use of an asset, both profit on capital and rent from land are unearned receipts or "rents" in a broader sense. Both are secured without effort, as is the physiocratic idea of the net product taken by the aristocracy for owning land and what the mills in Panama with their million-dollar profits secured beyond the costs of grinding the sugarcane.

My venture into Ricardo led me to confront my mental divide again. Ricardian reasoning attracted me for its elegance, but could deductive reason in economics be reconciled with contextual interpretation in anthropology? The two must be part of all economies, but how are they linked? The problem was unsolved, and I needed to see both from a larger perspective.

CHAPTER 5

# Colombia

Panama had been the northern part of Colombia until it separated in the early twentieth century with naval support from the United States government that wanted to build a canal. Prior studies of peasant life in Colombia resonated with the ethnography I gathered, and many of Panama's laws were adapted from the Colombian legal system. I wanted to know more about this source of Panama's culture.

In the early 1980s, Alberto Rivera wrote and finished his dissertation under my guidance. A Colombian by birth, he had studied an Indigenous group in the extreme north of Colombia. As we talked after his degree, our interests coalesced, and he invited me to study peasant life in Colombia. In early summer 1984, I went to Colombia from Cambridge, England, where our family had spent the earlier part of the year.

I did not imagine that this first visit would lead to four and a half years of intermittent research in Colombia and unusual experiences. Alberto and I worked together during summers, vacation breaks, and my released time from teaching. I could not take a single, extended period away, because I was chair of the Anthropology Department from 1984 to 1989, Roxane was teaching at Macalester College, and our daughters were into their teenage years that I did not want to miss. Each time I flew to Bogotá, and Alberto and I set out from there.

We decided to find two countryside villages where each of us would live to undertake comparative research. Within a few days of exploring northern Colombia together, a different idea emerged. We saw how learning and talking with each other during the fieldwork, and drawing on our different field experiences and personal backgrounds, led to insights and decided to try both joint fieldwork and cover a comparative area. Anthropology expects solitary research, but why adhere to the accepted image if an alternative is more interesting? We extended the research to Andean or highland culture from north to south in Colombia. Our focus became the house economy in the Andes.

Alberto was an ideal research partner. Always in good humor and optimistic, he has a strong yet friendly presence. Quick-witted and fast to pick up a topic, Alberto sensed what a person needed to hear, which served us well as we continually met people in our work.

Both of us enjoyed banter and soon fell into blaming the other for the missteps we shared, while neither of us forgot the mistakes of the other. The banter eased the tension of engaging new people and encountering difficult conditions from tires bursting as we drove, to lack of food and places to sleep, as well as frustration with opaque conversations in the field. Our conversations ranged from small or complex research issues to the larger impact of the US demand for illegal drugs that was tearing apart Colombia's social fabric.

On our first journey from Bogotá by car, we headed north through the plains or savanna and then eastward into the Andes. Our initial stopping place was the town of Soatá, which lies about 6,000 feet above sea level. We returned there several times over the years, because it was a meeting place for roads to the north and slightly east into even higher, more remote rural areas.

During our initial trip in the area, we spent hours following a narrow, dirt road that ended at a house whose front was a small store. An older peasant was sitting outside. He said that he lived further up the mountain where he raised crops, and Alberto talked him into letting us visit. Leaving the car and with packs on our backs, we climbed a narrow, rocky path until we reached our host's house on a very high plain. Made of mud walls with a thatch roof, it looked similar to those I knew in Panama. We sat under his overhanging roof, talked briefly about agriculture because he said little, and were shown to a storage room that adjoined his house and had a mud floor. We fashioned a bed of planks for our sleeping bags. The room had a few sacks of food, which looked nibbled, and in the middle of the night Alberto woke me and shone his flashlight on a rat crawling toward my ear.

Our host was up at 5:30 a.m. using his machete to clear a few weeds in the plantings he had adjacent to his house, but he was still not talkative. His companion said he was always up early because he liked to work in their small garden keeping it neat before he went to his fields. She offered coffee, and we trekked back downhill, while I ruminated about his care with the garden at his house and recalled the thrifty efforts of the peasants in Panama that gave them pride. How could I incorporate that into an account of local economy?

Descending the uneven path that led over rocks, we saw few people, except for one man with a twisted foot who was going up the trail carrying a large sack of potatoes on his shoulder. Given his disability and effort, I thought again of Panama and the city people who said rural folk are lazy. Sometime later back in Soatá, I spoke with a visiting nurse from Bogotá who said country folk "are lazy and careless," while I silently recalled the care our host on the high plain took with his house garden and the injured man hefting the potatoes. I began to think about the division between city and countryside with its reverberations of economic power.

We explored this northern region several times over the years where we met local folk here and there, and talked about their economy. The people raised maize, coffee, and tobacco depending on the immediate area. If the crops were different from Panama, the local economies seemed similar. Household groups raised crops for home consumption with leftovers taken to a market.

Deprivation and hardship throughout these areas were palpable. One night we stopped in a small town and found a back room in a small, single-story house where we stayed the night. In the morning we were offered breakfast. The meal, a large bowl of potato broth, was served in a small courtyard that opened to the street. I ate as much as I could and sat back. A small boy passing by in the street, looked in, spied my half-full bowl, and pointing to himself said, "Can I?" I got up from my chair. He climbed on and gobbled up the rest of my soup.

The second morning the woman set before us a more elaborate broth. Floating in the liquid were undercooked slices of pig meat with the dark skin still on and bristly hairs sticking out. I looked at the bubbles of fat floating across the broth's surface and then at Alberto. He looked at me, both of us looked down at the mix of lard, hairs, and chunks of skin, and then we looked to the street for help but saw no youngsters.

The woman came out from the kitchen, checking that we had everything and returned to the kitchen, but her dog stayed and lay at our feet. Without a word, we took turns dumping the soup on the cement floor, which the dog ate. It took some time, so we drank coffee and kept asking for refills of our cups. Each time she disappeared, we dumped.

The prior day I felt good about the hungry boy having his fill of my breakfast. This time, since our host was suspicious and the wet spots on the floor betrayed us, I felt ashamed at this rejection of her food, and even if that feeling was outweighed by the prospect of eating hairy pigskin suspended in bubbles of fat, I was disappointed with myself for not being a participatory anthropologist and more sensitive to the deprivation surrounding us.

***

Having started in the northern parts of Colombia, we enlarged the research area by going from north to south along the Andean strip and often doubled back. As we traveled by car along circuitous routes, I gazed at the architecture of rural houses and began to see related forms. The simplest peasant house is a square or rectangle with a kitchen and one connected room. The walls are plastered mud. One side has an overhanging roof under which people sit to have light and protection from the heat as they prepare food or talk. This house from above looks like the letter I.

Other houses have an L-shape with the two sections at right angles to one another. The roof may overhang both sides of the inner angle. Less frequently, I saw rectangle-shaped houses that have one open end. These dwellings have a partially enclosed patio with the roof overhang inside the three sides. The fourth form is a four-sided square with an enclosed patio that is not visible from the outside. It has at least two overhangs above the patio. The invariant right-angle architecture intrigued me stylistically and because the roofing requires skill with a plumb line (as I saw when Jacinto built his house in Panama). The enclosed form suggests, perhaps, a move to privacy and holding or keeping within that fits the broader way of life. I surmised that peasant houses were modeled after the four-sided hacienda, and with wealth, a peasant house might be enlarged through the shapes to the great house or hacienda.

Haciendas no longer functioned as large house economies. We visited several haciendas to see the architecture and reconstruct in our minds the style of life. Some were plantations devoted to raising a cash crop, one or two were countryside homes for the wealthy, and some were abandoned. My hypothesis that great houses were models for the peasant house and its growth remained in my head, because I was never able to verify it with historical information.

Outside the town of Covarachía in the north, we came across an abandoned hacienda with many of its out buildings still standing. We could see from the partly standing structures that the full hacienda consisted of a great house, chapel, storehouses, quarters for workers, and plots for the peasant house economies that helped supply the hacienda. Walking through the dilapidated great house we found it had many square courtyards all connected as if the basic square form had been joined one to another, perhaps over time, but we never located sketches or plans of the hacienda.

A family had owned the hacienda for generations and used the land for raising crops, but some of the descendants had turned to the drug trade that was more remunerative. When authorities closed in, the owners fled to the United States, and the government seized the hacienda and divided its large land mass into plots for peasant use. In the later 1980s, when we were there, the drug trade in Colombia centered on raising and sending marijuana to the United States, but the transport of cocaine from the southern border of Colombia to the Caribbean was becoming significant as we soon found.

Driving along a dirt road in the north, we stopped at a collection of houses, encountered a young man, and asked him a few questions. "You have to speak with the local leader," he said and pointed. "He lives down the hill." He began walking and waved for us to follow. I carried a clipboard with a tablet of notes and a large camera. The teenager walked rapidly, as did Alberto, and I had difficulty keeping up, especially because my boots kept slipping on the wet ground. We came to a narrow brook that they crossed by jumping from rock to rock. I stepped more gingerly and slipped on a wet rock. Falling backward I held the notes and camera above me and landed in a pile of cow dung in the water. Getting up and twisting around, I saw that the cow's leavings covered my behind and smelled, but I was pleased at saving the notes and camera.

The others were waiting, and as we walked on, I wobbled my behind and tried to shake off the leavings. The sloping plain had no trees on which I might rub and deposit the stuff. Eventually we reached the mud and thatch house of the hamlet head. Beckoning us inside, he offered us benches, but I dared not sit and kept moving with my back to the walls of his house. I do not know if my smell influenced him, but he did not take kindly to us, would scarcely talk, and instructed us to see the mayor of the district.

Trudging back, I crossed the stream by walking in the water. In the car I tore paper from my notebook to cover the seat, and we backtracked to a very small town where the mayor was located. In his tiny office I still smelled and sat on the edge of a chair. The mayor was abrupt, did not grasp the nature of our work, and said that strangers could not enter the district.

Alberto grew increasingly incensed. "I have the right as a Colombian to travel anywhere," he blurted.

The two argued back and forth becoming ever more heated.

"I'll call the police," the mayor said, "and the two of you will go to jail."

I pulled my notes and camera to my chest. I was not concerned about landing in jail, at least for a short time, but was worried about what they would do with my field notes that were in Spanish and English as well as the film I had saved from the cow's droppings. Nudging Alberto, I kept saying in English, "Cool it, man." The mayor explained that his district had become a passageway for drugs and had been ordered to expel all strangers, so retreat was our move. Back in the car, I kept changing my paper cushion for the remainder of the day.

I had a more serious casualty a few days later. One evening we found ourselves in a small town that might have had tourist aspirations. Looking about we saw an old six-floor, cement block hotel with no lights showing. We entered to find the thirty-year-old proprietress sitting in the dark lobby. She said the hotel was empty, and we could select whichever room we wished. On the first floor the windows in each room were missing or the glass was cracked with jagged edges showing. We climbed to find the same at each level and always with beds that had no coverings. Finally, we settled with our sleeping bags in a top floor room with only partially broken windows that gave some protection from the wind. The cold in this mountainous area was heightened by the lack of doors and heating in the rooms that had no lights.

In the morning we saw nobody about, and the hotel doors were locked. Making our way through the empty kitchen to the basement, we found a door that opened to a walled-in courtyard.

Nodding at the wall, I said "Let's find breakfast," so we decided to scale the wall. I jumped and grabbed the top, which was a mistake. I made it over, but still cold from the night, I cracked something in my back that left me wincing in pain and mute for days. A few years later I began to have back problems that eventually led to surgeries. Doctors continually asked how I had injured my back, but I shall never know whether the United States medical system profited from this fieldwork casualty. I do know that when we returned to the hotel, after finding coffee and rolls elsewhere, the proprietress was angry with us for not staying for breakfast that would have been scrounged from the empty kitchen. We left, and I popped aspirin for days.

***

We used a car extensively for the fieldwork. Alberto would find a friend or a friend of a friend or a distant relative who would lend us an old one. I was convinced that he invented the connections, because he would first find out whom the person knew and then come up with a link.

We learned to carry extra tires because most of the roads were a mix of dirt and large stones, and we punctured tires regularly. Driving one-lane rocky tracks around mountains with corners that had sharp falloffs and blind curves with trucks sometimes approaching was dangerous and tiring. Occasionally we saw small buses with one tire off the edge struggling to get back on the road. At the side of roads, we saw small crosses signaling someone's demise at that spot. I spelled Alberto driving, but after a time he did it all, for he was accustomed to the roads and could talk as we drove, which I could not.

Each small car, often an old Renault, became our office where we endlessly conversed. Alberto knew the regions of the country, their ecology, and much of their history from his education in Colombia. I was trying to make sense of the local economies.

We developed a fieldwork technique. As we drove through an area seeing people in a field, at a house, on the road, or at a collection of houses, we stopped to talk with them or be referred to someone else. I took notes continuously during these interviews. On leaving, we drove a short distance, stopped, and sat in the dirt or on a boulder, completing the notes about what we had seen and heard. Back in the car we compared what each of us had learned, often with slightly different interpretations. At times, we turned around and went back to find our interviewee and clarify our understanding, and sometimes that did not help.

In a marketplace one afternoon the two of us met a frail, white-haired old man sitting with a wheelbarrow that was filled with dried sugarcane cakes called *panela*. I had watched them being made in Panama and then in Colombia. Having purchased a batch from peasant producers, the old man was selling them in the market mostly to pass the time seeing and meeting people. As we talked, he told us about working for a hacienda in the 1930s and 1940s, which caught our attention when he called it "slavery." In those years he would move from hacienda to hacienda, because he had no land himself. We asked, "What were your obligations at the hacienda?"

His response was muddy. One of us heard "three work days each week" for access to a plot of land where he could grow food, but the other heard "five days a week and food" for a plot. Alberto had recorded the interview and we later listened to it, but the recording was hard to hear and his voice was so faint we could not decipher his words. At the time, we were trying to figure out the difference between paying workers in cash or in food, how the people translated one to the other, and how the payments were linked to the work performed, because we were encountering vestiges of the two forms of payment elsewhere. Alas, his historical knowledge remained a puzzle, because we could not find him on returning, although hearing first-hand about servitude at haciendas in southern Colombia was captivating in both senses of the word.

***

Alberto knew the local expressions of the people far better than I. Sometimes he connected a phrase to something his grandmother had said, while I compared the information to Panama. Alberto knew my Panama work, so these comparisons and conversations with others and between us improved our interpretations. In the car we also talked about what we knew and did not know, which gave us new questions. After a while, we began to tell people in one area what others elsewhere had said to get their reflections on those responses.

The talks between Alberto and myself went on over meals and at bedtime. We were learning the precise language the people used for the economy of the house. Again, and again, we heard the word "strength" (or force) and distinguished it from the people's use of "power" (or might). I recalled that Panamanians said rice gives strength and men would clasp and bend a bicep to indicate strength as they uttered the word "oomph." I thought they were talking about physical strength. Twenty years later in Colombia when I remembered this material, which still puzzled me, I understood what the people had been saying.

Strength in the crops they eat, the rural Colombians told us, comes from the trees, the sun, the wind, and the earth. Human work puts these elements together, but work itself does not create strength. Like a barber, as I had learned in Panama, humans do not generate something extra through their work. They are craftsmen or artisans who compose strength for use by humans.

Strength, I now saw, meant more than physical force. It is the energy of life or vital energy. Human work, drawing on strength, helps yield strength in the crops that are raised by arranging the four elements which compose it in agriculture. Crops are part of a flow of strength that runs from preparing the land, to seeding, weeding, harvesting, eating, and starting again.

The current of strength not only connects people to the environment, which provides its elements, but to others in the house who share the same strength through the food they jointly eat just as they mutually expend their strength producing that food. One person's vital energy becomes part of others' strength through his work and their consumption of that strength in food, so that a house is composed of people related by kinship and conjugality and a flow of shared strength.

Vital energy also connects houses because it is transferred between them when one person works for another. One person's expended strength helps compose the vital energy of others through the food he helps to produce for them, while their strength becomes his through the work or food offered in return. A house shares and receives vital energy through the back and forth of work. In attenuated and transitory form, strength provides connections in a community through work and food, and in a junta to build a house itself. I hesitate to call strength a currency, for it is not counted, and money is not ingested, but strength is like a current or flow starting in a house, radiating outward, and disappearing to reappear.

When I realized that vital energy connects people, I finally understood the final night of the wake in Panama when people exit the house of the deceased, extinguish their candles with a puff of breath and reshape the physical structure to exclude the bed of the deceased. They are "saying" or expressing that the deceased no longer is part of their flow of vital energy. His strength or "air," as they symbolically said, has left.

This same understanding of strength brought back another memory from Panama. Six years after fieldwork, when I returned for a visit and showed our neighbors a picture of our first daughter, Rebecca, many said, "She looks Panamanian." I thought they were teasing me, because Roxane had stayed a few weeks in the village after I left to complete her study, and a single woman was always suspected of having lovers. Now I realized they were connecting our daughter to them, because I understood their idea that the earth and other elements provide the strength of life through food. Roxane and I were eating food from Panama's soil shortly before Rebecca's conception, so she embodied some of their vital energy and was connected to them.

An economy built on flows of vital energy provides a sobering critique of market notions. It contrasts with our idea that economy consists of exchanging goods, services, and money. An economy of markets separates people, while an economy of vital energy connects them. The vital energy notion also presents a different vision of market exploitation, because the cash crops a people raise, whether maize, potatoes, or another comestible, send vital energy to others in return for a lesser amount in the food they are able to purchase with their monetary returns.

Visualizing economy as a flow of vital energy also undercuts market notions that growth is good and more growth is better, because the natural world has limited potential for providing vital energy, except for the endless amount provided by the sun. The people's model of economy, based on what the environment can yield for human life, offers a critique of our quest for an expanding gross domestic product, which occurs at the expense of natural resources.

The people's account of "production" in Colombia and Panama is very different from ours that emphasizes the productive role of labor. It reminded me of the Physiocrats who attributed productivity only to the land and other natural resources. But how did physiocratic thinking end up in parts of Latin America? Did Spanish-speaking Jesuits transmit it? Whatever the origin of the peasants' ideas, their understanding of labor's place in economy took me very far from a Marxist interpretation that the effort of labor creates value and from market economics in which labor, land, capital, and demand determine market value.

This local model of material life also led me to a different understanding of economy's place in Panama and Colombia, for I now saw it as both separate from but encompassed by divine power. The flow of strength enabling life differs from the current of spirit that also enables life in the same way that earthly parents who are connected to their children through the bodily strength they provide are different from godparents who are connected to their godchildren through the spiritual tie they offer. In both cases earthly life is sustained by material elements, but it is empowered by spirit, for strength is encompassed by power. Thus, I ultimately came to see the everyday economies in Panama and Colombia as representing something more than material life. They embody God's power that makes earthly strength possible. As economies that refer to something other than themselves (or to rational choice), they are ritual economies. My slow realization that economy might be a symbolic construction rather than the foundation for symbolic life was accentuated when Alberto and I explored another, central notion in the people's economy and suddenly reached a luminous conclusion when we heard a "voice in the air."

***

Alberto and I kept hearing the word "base" as we traveled. We had been making progress in understanding how a house economy works and had bits and pieces of the picture but no overall view until one morning in northern Colombia. We were drinking coffee, eating bread, and conversing about "the base," when our fragmentary talk fell together. We sensed that "making a base" was a central idea in the people's economy.

We left the food, paid, jumped up, got in the car, drove to the nearest field we could find, saw a campesino weeding in his field with a machete, got out and began asking him questions about the land, the crops, and the house. Unfazed by a surprise visit from two people he had never seen, he confirmed that the base sustains a house, and includes the house plus the land, the growing crops, the food stored, and all the materials needed for living including tools. He stood there, spreading his arms, swiveling his body with fingers outstretched, and said, "This is my base, all of it. Every house has a base."

My work on metaphors and models of economy came to mind. When our informant said, "This is my base," he meant more than the physical foundation of the house. The physical house with its base provided the image for talking and thinking about material life. Food, clothes, tools, and even the house compose the base of material life. The base of a house is both its bottom part and the foundation of each house economy, for it is the vital energy that people have accumulated for living.

Other pieces of the puzzle fit. The people say that goods come "in" and go "out" the doors, even when they do no such thing. The "in" and "out" the doors refers to the crops, tools, and animals that move in and out of the house economy itself. Food raised by the house, even if outside the dwelling, is "in" the doors, while crops sold, go "out the doors," with the cash or goods received coming back "in" the doors. If the house economy fails to sustain its base, the people say, "the house is ruined, it is in ruins," even when the physical structure is standing.

Hearing these expressions in Colombia reminded me of another puzzle from Panama. When I talked with men there after a day of work, and they spoke about being tired or weary (*cansado*) but would add, "I am not *estropeado* (broken down or damaged) and will work tomorrow." Their words may have resonated with the first and second laws of energy but they were referring to their vital energy that would be restored by the base. Neither they nor the house was in ruins.

***

As Alberto and I continued driving and visiting, we talked about the base in an expanded sense as a heritage of ideas and practices on which people rely, such as the ways of doing agriculture in the countryside that are seen, learned, and slowly revised. I recalled the basement room in King's College that was filled with silver and suddenly saw it not as a collection of valuable gifts to the college that potentially could be sold but as part of its base, like the Chapel that King's sustains as part of its identity. The base of the house in Panama and Colombia, accumulated and fashioned by its inhabitants for their way of living, expresses their identity, as we witnessed that early day of fieldwork when we stayed overnight with the man who arose at 5:30 a.m. to tend the garden plot at his house in the highlands.

I then began to see that the word, hacienda, from the word *hacer*, which means to make or do, could be interpreted as the final making or the finishing of a base, which fit my earlier image of the hacienda as a making from the small, square-shaped house.

With these speculations, we kept filling out our picture of the local economy. It had taken time, because the concept of the base erases our market categories that separate resources from goods and humans as in our notions of land, capital, and labor. The physical base of a house is visible yet not separate from the house because it is a part of what people have made as in the hacienda. Did the campesino notion of the base provide a critique of our idea of capital as a separate thing to be bought and sold? I recalled Sraffa's letter in the King's College library with his comparison of modern economics to theology and debunking of the idea of capital. Is the notion of capital an abstraction from that of an economy's base?

Verification may not be the proper word for our methodology of probing, asking, backtracking, looking for patterns, and then trying our picture on others. Philosophers of science talk about hypotheses and falsification in relation to scientific findings. They usually do not defend the idea of verification or confirmation. Our technique was at variance with this more accepted method of accruing knowledge. We had been challenging our picture by continually trying it on new people for their thoughts and then adjusting it. Of course, we had to weigh what they said and had to be careful not to elicit answers we sought, which was not hard because we usually did not know the answers in advance. We also had to consider whether the picture we were drawing was a delusion of ours or a delusion of the campesinos that we were adopting. So, verification with falsification, and revisions, partly captures what we were doing. Further encounters gave me confidence that we were on the right path.

One day on the road we saw an older man carrying a sack of tubers on his back. Stopping, we offered him a ride. He thanked us and got in the narrow back seat. We asked where he was going, which was some miles ahead. For the moment, he was in our rolling office, so we asked him questions and told him our impressions about what we were seeing.

"Why do people say 'May it come up well' when they are planting?" I began.

"It is God's will, his power, to make it grow. But you have to work, to use your strength."

"What is the base?" I asked.

"I am carrying this sack home for our base," he answered.

Again and again, we tried our new language on him, and when we stopped to let him out, he turned and said, "It's so nice to talk to intellectuals like you who understand."

Another time we saw workers digging up potatoes in a field. We drove into the field and stopped. They gathered around the car in front, on both sides, and in back. We rolled our windows down and began to talk, hearing voices from people we could not even see. This time I began to pose "physiocratic" questions.

"If all strength comes from the earth, what value does a woman have who does not work the earth?"

"She is assisting in gaining strength. Men and women's work have equal value."

One Sunday morning in northern Colombia we were bumping along a dry dirt road not knowing where we were but trusting that the road led somewhere. Ahead, on the left side of the road, we saw a group of people standing near a stick and thatch house. We stopped, went up, greeted them, and noticed they were gathered in front of a rounded outdoor oven made of dried mud with a small opening at the front. We had seen these ovens before but this was the first time we saw one in use. A family was baking bread and had invited friends to eat the hot product. It was a chance to try our stuff, and we went through some of the now familiar ideas. Soon, I thought of a question that until then had been only partially formed in my mind. We knew about the concept of the base and that it took materials or a base to make a base, so I asked, "If it takes a base to make a base, from where did the first base come?"

I had no answer in mind and was greeted with silence. We repeated the question and still no response. I thought my question must have been poorly framed, when suddenly, a woman at the back of the group said, "The Garden of Eden – Adam and Eve."

I was too surprised to respond, for her answer completed our understanding. She was saying that God made the world with his might (*el poder*) and humans (Cain and Abel, farming and herding) compose it to have the strength (*la fuerza*) for living. Other voices completed the story talking about God's gift of sustenance on Sunday, and the human provision of sustenance during the week. A lone voice in the air had confirmed our understanding of their world.

***

I began hearing voices in my head as Alberto continued to do the driving. I had no plan to dredge up memories, but sitting and looking at the changing landscape of mountains, cliffs, and shimmering green, and sometimes not registering the view, my mind strayed to earlier writers in economics and economic history. One day, musing about the people's idea of the base, I recalled what John Maynard Keynes termed "a fundamental psychological law," the "precautionary motive," which is to save or hold back from consumption as a safeguard against unexpected events. Interest paid on savings, he argued, is the reward to the saver for parting with his money holdings and their use by someone else. We were not traveling in a cash economy, and the local notion of the base encompassed more than money, but I realized that the psychology of keeping as a precaution was common across economies, from a house based to a market focused one. We were traveling through an economic zone that was different from anything I had experienced in my youth or read about but increasingly understandable, and perhaps it represented a precursor to the one I learned growing up and in business school. My father's pleasure in being thrifty despite his immersion in the market world was an expression of this psychology of keeping. The glittering silver objects I had seen in the *base*ment of King's College two decades previously were symbols of its continuing identity but also cognizance of an uncertain future. Had Keynes who ate and drank from these vessels viewed them this way in the early part of the century?

I recalled a famous phrase from Keynes:

> The ideas of economists and political philosophers, both when they are right and when they are wrong, are more powerful than is commonly understood. Indeed the world is ruled by little else. Practical men, who believe themselves to be quite exempt from any intellectual influence, are usually the slaves of some defunct economist. ([1936] 2017: 383)

Keynes's sentences, I thought, applied more to the "ideas" of people like those we were meeting in the outlands of Colombia than to past economists and political philosophers to whom he was referring. We were wandering in echoes of an intellectual history from Aristotle, to the Schoolmen, Aquinas, the Physiocrats, Turgot, and others, but from where did they get their ideas? I was not a scholar of all this thought or its on-the-ground history and awaited my return to the United States to consult some texts, but my mind exploded on discovering these unknown connections between the Old World and the New World, and that ethnography could provide clues to our own written and practical history.

One day, as I was ruminating about these historical echoes, we stopped at the top of a hill to look down and watch a man plowing a field. Two oxen were drawing a wooden yoke with a metal-tipped plow. The driver, holding the plow behind, was singing to the pair, urging and guiding them with reins. The scene could have been from Roman times, except for the steel tipped plow, and I longed for a movie camera to capture this ancient moment in the 1980s.

Other historical bits and pieces fueled my imagination. One afternoon we reached a remote plateau in the mountains of southern Colombia. Below us was a large field of potatoes being harvested by a group of workers dragging sacks to hold the tubers when my thoughts suddenly bounced from esoteric economics to religion.

I had been musing about the house economy and about ecology with their common root in the Greek word *oikos*. As we had traveled upward, the ecology was slowly shifting as were the crops from garden vegetables, to maize, to potatoes. I was not giving as much attention to this relation between the environs and the crops as I might have, except for noticing that what people could plant and raise for consumption was not only shifting but often becoming more and more constricted as we reached higher altitudes. At the plateau, where only potatoes could be raised, we reached a "one commodity economy." I knew the expression was most often used for an economy dependent on a single product for sale, such as oil, rubber, or cotton, and often in a context of colonial control and markets. This mountain zone populated with house economies was different. Of course, the people had to sell or barter their one commodity for other goods, with the effort of transporting it down the mountain, but it also meant that the single good had to be a mainstay of the diet, just as rice was eaten three times a day in Panama.

We made our way from the road down to the workers. They were about to take a late morning break, and we sat with them as each brought out cooked potatoes for the midmorning repast. As we talked, I was offered some boiled potatoes garnished with a small red pepper, which was my participation in a one commodity economy if only on the consumption side.

After the meal, we returned to the car and watched the workers slowly moving along one row and then another, dragging burlap bags to hold the potatoes they were digging up using sticks and trowels. Some rows were not being harvested, so I counted the harvested ones and saw that nine were cleaned of potatoes while the tenth was left. Puzzled but with an inkling, we descended again, and I asked a man. The tenth row, he said, was left for gathering by the church. It was the tithe, revealing the hold of religious practices. I never saw the practice in Panama or elsewhere in Colombia.

The similarities between the Old World and the New World led me to wonder how this history had reached across the ocean. Who brought the customs and ideas—Jesuit teachers, landowners, or elite thinkers? Undertaking research on this topic would require a lifetime, if it were possible, and with these few bits and pieces of ethnography, I could only imagine that history.

Twenty years after the Colombia research was completed, a similar puzzle about the historical and cultural similarity of economic models across gaps in history and space returned to me. I was overseeing a team project in six countries of Eastern Europe and Asia that had been under Soviet rule until 1989. The researchers, who worked in rural areas, found economic practices and ideas that resonated with the material from Latin America, although these regions had been under Soviet domination since the end of World War II, but I could understand many practices in these post-socialist areas—especially the presence of house economies—and able to suggest lines of inquiry to the researchers. Their findings were not point-by-point similar to the practices and verbal explanations in Latin America, but the geographic spread, historical persistence of ideas about economy, and similarities between the Old World and the New World were tantalizing and slightly validated my research begun forty years earlier.

My learning through conversations in the field and memories did not stop after leaving the countryside. During the few times we came back to Bogotá, and on my arrival and departure from the United States, I stayed with Alberto's mother. Her family has a long history in the country, which I could see from the old family portraits on her dining room walls. Through her stories about the people in the portraits and their politics I heard an intimate side of Colombian history.

One Sunday afternoon seven of her cousins and other relatives came for a visit. Dressed in dark suits and semi-formal wear, they sat around the dining room table. A French press coffee pot was brought out and the coffee was ceremoniously brewed. We slowly drank the coffee, and I listened as the family, all older people, made conversation for three hours. Sometimes the talk was about personal or shared stories from the past. Other times the talk mixed current news with Colombian history.

Watching and listening, I recalled the Spanish custom of holding a *tertulia* in which a group gathers to talk art, politics, history, or contemporary affairs. Such gatherings are disappearing in the face of television and other attractions, but that Sunday in Bogotá I was listening to elegant Spanish spoken among kinfolk who held a conversation for its own sake. I had learned to have purposeful talk. Their exchanges sustained relationships and represented a heritage that re-enforced identity.

A different experience in Bogotá also brought past and present together. Alberto and I had decided to travel east from Bogotá to the savanna below the city's escarpment. The savanna led southward to the Amazon Rainforest, and I wanted to see peasant life in this area at the border of the Amazon.

An older relative, Alberto told me, had traveled the region by horseback fifty years earlier. One evening we set out along a Bogotá boulevard past grand houses set back from the avenue until we reached a large, old home. On the front porch a group of teenagers was gathered, drinking and talking. We entered the house. In the front room and the next were more young people dancing and drinking. (I was almost forty, and they looked young to me.) Passing through these rooms into a darker one with old furniture, the noise subsided. We entered another darker room, and I felt I was slowly moving away from the present. On the room's far side, Alberto knocked on a door and we entered a last room at the back of the house. Table lamps provided flickering yellow light. Sitting in a wooden swivel chair at a roll-top desk facing a wall was a pale, older man wearing a dark suit, white shirt, and black tie.

He was Alberto's distant uncle. Pictures and photographs of his journeys from more than a half-century earlier adorned the walls of his room. He pivoted to greet us, and we talked. Alberto's uncle pointed to the pictures and told us how he had traveled by horseback throughout the country many years before. We did not learn much to help our research, but his talk about past life and our spatial movement through the house from front to back, light to dark, and young to old evoked for me the historical layers of Colombian life and their melding. The moment crystallized my growing sense about our research in the countryside. It was current and a historical excavation.

The book that Alberto and I produced from the research was entitled *Conversations in Colombia* (1990) in which I connected the Colombian peasant model of economy to leading European ones prior to Adam Smith. My pulse had been quickened because many Colombian customs from the house economy to religious beliefs and practices resonated with rural life in Panama.

***

After meeting Alberto's uncle, we descended to the plains east of the city, found a collective ride, and set out south and eastward. After ten hours driving in hot weather on a narrow mud road through the sparsely populated savanna where cattle occasionally grazed, the driver stopped and refused to go further. We walked with our packs hoping to find a settlement on the road. Eventually, we found ourselves at the base camp of the Colombian Summer Institute of Linguistics (SIL), the same missionary group with whose team I had stayed across the mountain divide in Panama. The Colombian encampment was large and encircled by barbed wire.

Permitted to enter, we were surrounded by American teenagers riding motor scooters. Passing by a landing strip, I saw three airplanes. Each had three decals. One said US, the second was inscribed AID, and the third displayed the insignia of the Colombian air force. At the office of the encampment, we learned the SIL had forty teams spread throughout Colombia who were serviced by plane from the plains. I wondered why the US, AID, and the Colombian government were supporting religious missionaries.

The director invited us to stay the night. In the dining hall the talk was in English, the cooks were American, and we ate hamburgers and french fries. The food was flown in from the United States and featured no local purchases. After dinner, a screen was erected and a recent Hollywood film was shown. We went to bed and in the morning left this island of the United States that reminded me of the Canal Zone. Ten years later, the enclave was invaded and destroyed by one of the Colombian militant groups.

Stymied by car, we returned to Bogotá to make a second attempt at reaching the southern end of the savanna by air. We climbed aboard an aged two-engine DC3. I last rode one thirty-five years before, and this one sounded older than that. Because it was used for cargo and devoid of seats, we sat along the walls and held onto straps as air pockets buffeted us.

Landing at San José del Guaviare, we found ourselves in a small town on the northern edge of the Amazon. Walking with our packs, we first encountered campesinos chopping down the forest for planting. The agriculture was familiar, and the people looked and sounded like many we had encountered in northern sections of the country. Most of the people had moved from overworked land in other parts of the country in search of plots for raising food. These farmers were slowly razing the jungle and moving further into the Amazon forest.

Passing by a small hamlet populated by agriculturalists and finally reaching a river that fed the Amazon River, we found a man with a narrow, flat-bottomed, motorized wooden boat slightly larger than a canoe and arranged to go downstream. Going downriver, we saw small Indigenous villages containing a few huts but no people. Toward the end of the day, we stopped where a solitary man, dressed in rags, was sitting at the top of a bank near houses. We climbed up, joined him and talked in Spanish, which was not his first language. With a faltering voice, he told us "incoming agriculturalists are destroying the forest, and now I cannot survive by hunting, fishing and seeding. I may move downriver, although I do not know where." His slumping body and shoulders mirrored his words.

Today, when thinking about environmental devastation and its human consequences, this final encounter and its image come to mind, for the man's predicament was the result of an expanding market frontier and a chain of displacements: small-scale subsistence agriculturalists in accessible, fertile locations are dislodged by capitalized farmers. The agriculturalists move to find forest that they can fell and burn to raise their crops. The forest dwellers are displaced as their habitat disappears and must move, and their society withers. This domino effect seems ceaseless.

Traveling through this sequence of environmental devastation, human movement, and immiseration brought back a memory from Panama. My friend, Miguel, left the village when its land was taken over by the new sugarcane mill to have supplies of the crop, a change to which I made a contribution. To find forest and land for raising food, he fled to the Darien jungle and joined the human flow cutting the pristine forest. As I asked my father that Sunday afternoon long ago, "Where does it stop?" We returned to Bogotá after this trip.

***

One other time we traveled by airplane. Alberto and I flew to Pasto, which is the capital of the southern state, Nariño. We had been stymied driving there because the route would have taken us through areas controlled by guerrilla groups and drug lords. The Pasto airfield, located higher than the city, which lies at 8,000 feet, is a small mountain plateau with steep drops on all sides. I hardly noticed its positioning on the flight in, although I did see that the plane ran to the end of the strip before it stopped with nothing but a drop ahead. When we finished our research in the area, we returned to the airport for the flight back to Bogotá. We waited and waited, because the strong winds blew airplanes off the runway. When we were cleared to leave, I wet a finger, held it up to test the wind, would have said a prayer had I believed in its efficacy, and climbed aboard.

While we were in the area, Alberto found an acquaintance who lent us his old Land Rover. The offer was generous, because a Land Rover was the perfect vehicle for our travels. The steering was loose and the vehicle rattled but served its purpose as we traveled rough roads up and down hills and in thick forests.

On the fifth day in the outlands, we were driving through a hilly forest on a one-lane, dirt track. I was sitting in the front seat and began to smell gas, but Alberto claimed the gauge indicated we were fine. We rode to the top of a hill. There, a woman stood, frantically yelling and waving for us to stop. We did and discovered a man lying on his back by the road. Embedded in his chest was a knife.

Agreeing to drive them to the nearest town with a doctor that was hours away, we loaded him on his back through the door at the rear of the Land Rover with the knife still in his chest and left the door open so his feet could stick out.

I got back in my front seat and Alberto turned the key. Nothing. He turned the key again and pumped the gas with no better result. After the third time all still remained quiet in the back, except for low groans, and Alberto said to me, "We'll have to push it."

I went to the front, pushed the car, hopped in, and we rolled backward down the hill. When the Land Rover gathered speed near the bottom, Alberto yanked the floor shift into reverse to start the motor. The lever flew out backward and the car jerked to a halt. The man slid out the back door and landed with a thud on the road. He cried out and the woman screamed. In the front seat I recalled the unintended disasters in the French film *Mr. Hulot's Holiday*, thinking "this catastrophe will come to an end." Both of us got out and lifted the hardly conscious, moaning man into the car. Alberto put the lever in place and tried starting repeatedly with no result.

About forty minutes later another Land Rover came along and stopped. We siphoned gas from it, the driver hooked a chain to our front, hauled us up the hill, and the motor started. The other Land Rover took the man, and still smelling gas, we proceeded, but after a few miles the car sputtered. Turning off the road we ran it into the forest and walked with our backpacks. As darkness fell, a small truck came along, stopped for us to climb into the open back, and carried us to the nearest town where we stayed for the night. The next day when we called Alberto's friend to report about his Land Rover, he said to leave it in the forest.

Now we were stuck. Wandering about the town, we found a garage, saw it had an old, small Renault, convinced the owner to rent it to us, and off we went into the backlands. Two nights later in another town, after a long day of talking with people, we parked the car below the window of the second-floor room where we had arranged to stay. About 4:00 a.m., I jerked awake at a screech and crunch of metal and went to the window. Looking down as Alberto slept, I saw a small bus pull away from the street side of the car. Muttering profanities, I thought, "It won't do any good to go down and look," and went back to bed.

In the morning we discovered that the left rear of the car was smashed. We found a garage that vowed to fix it and passed two days in the town while the mechanics pounded out the damage, matched the brown color of the car and repainted it. Mobile again, we journeyed out for more fieldwork and finally returned the car to its owners in the first town. They circled the car several times, sensing something was awry and asking questions, but soon away we went.

***

Car mishaps were not the only travel experiences that caught my eye. Small happenings when I flew from Colombia to the United States were symptomatic of the international relations affecting the entire nation from its banking center in Bogotá to its physical and economic periphery where we were working. Flying to the United States from Bogotá through Miami, I sat next to a Colombian. He owned pasture in the north (his brother's ranch adjoined his, so I assumed a larger tract had been inherited). They worried about being kidnapped for ransom, but if they did not live on the farms, they would not be able to keep cattle, which would be stolen without their presence. He was traveling to Miami and back only to deposit a stack of Colombian checks at "the Chase" and explained he wanted to get his money out of Colombia for security, did not trust the postal service, and could make money by changing it to dollars and saving it in the United States as the Colombian peso was falling relative to the dollar. Under the policy of Ronald Reagan, who was president at the time, he did not have to pay taxes on the interest he earned in the United States and was avoiding Colombian taxes as well. He also was protecting against being kidnapped by having no money in Colombia to pay ransom. On the back of an envelope, he showed me that by the combination of the changing exchange rate, interest received, and avoiding taxes in the United States and Colombia he was gaining 35 percent annually on his money by flying one day every other month to the Chase in Miami and depositing his checks there.

I participated in a border crossing of a different type. At the time of fieldwork, Colombian coffee was considered the best in the world and was far less expensive than United States coffee that we bought in tin containers. On my last trip to Colombia in the late 1980s, I brought an empty suitcase, bought hermetically sealed one-kilo bags of ground coffee, and put the bags in the suitcase. With the purchase in Colombia, I was saving enough to pay for my airfare and have better coffee for a year, but plan and result do not always match. When I reached customs in the United States, an agent opened the suitcase, brought out a knife and punched holes in all the bags to taste the contents as he searched for a forbidden substance. Finding only coffee, he let my suitcase through, but the coffee lost its flavor, I lost my savings, and I had finished the Colombia research.

CHAPTER 6

# Excursions

During the 1980s and the 1990s, I was drawn into academic responsibilities. Fulfilling departmental, collegiate, and university duties as well as reviewing for journals and presses made it increasingly difficult to carry out field research, and our daughters were in their teens and Roxane was teaching, but I was able to expand my knowledge of economic history and the history of economics. Turning to Aristotle, medieval notions of the just price, the economics of Anne Robert Jacques Turgot and Marquis de Mirabeau, John Locke, Adam Smith, the mercantilists and bullionists, Walter of Henley, and others did not provide a unified framework for economic anthropology but did help illuminate the ethnographies I was reading as it sharpened my understanding of economy. I continued to be influenced by Karl Polanyi, by Thorstein Veblen (1922) on workmanship, and by Denis Diderot (1751) on "artisanship." The reading had little relevance outside academia, but I once applied a small portion of this learning when called to jury duty.

## The Juror

When the judge threw me out of the courtroom, I was not surprised, because the defense and prosecution had discussed my dismissal. But his decisiveness was humbling.

I had been summoned to jury service with the warning that I would be arrested if I did not appear. Owing to teaching conflicts, I postponed the original date, but my time had arrived. I wanted, however, to see the proceedings and was proud to serve, because I thought that jury duty was a citizen's right and responsibility. Probably, it was this overweening righteousness linked to my brand of anthropology that produced the defense lawyer's outburst and my dismissal. I also had not anticipated that allegiance to the Constitution and to anthropology would make a combustible mix.

Jury service begins each Monday morning. My first mistake was to book a flight returning to Minneapolis from New York for Sunday evening. The airplane was hit by lightning and lost its electrical systems, so I spent the night near the New York airport, left early the next morning, and arrived late at the courthouse. I missed the jurors' orientation session and instructional film, and always felt a step behind the others.

About one hundred of us had been called for the week, and we filled a basement room. My observations were confirmed by the others: the vast majority were white and retired or employed in white-collar jobs, although gender mixed. I wondered at the imbalance of ethnicity and wealth, but jurors are randomly selected from voting lists.

Our windowless room had telephones—usually occupied by businesspeople—several computers, televisions, and newspapers. But it was hard not to feel imprisoned. I had brought my book manuscript, and in the subsequent days spent many hours revising it. Being paid $30 a day for juror service and daily anticipations about lunch gave special spice to my academic work.

On Thursday after lunch, I was working on the final chapter when the supervisor called out thirty names including mine. I had already been called twice, but the cases were settled before reaching the jury, and this one seemed different. We knew that calling a large number of potential jurors meant a serious case would be heard, and I had hoped to make it to the weekend to be excused from service in the following week. So, in a somber mood, we were herded into a large, padded elevator and taken to an upper floor.

Outside the courtroom, we were each given a seventeen-page questionnaire to complete. I quickly answered the questions about education, work, salary, and family; but the "yes" or "no" queries about race and the justice system made me feel uneasy. In the margins, I penned something about race as a cultural concept, and when trying to answer whether a "high proportion" of legal offenders are African Americans, I wrote about who defines crime, enforces the laws, and makes the judgments; and about statistical proportions as well as the prosecution of white-collar crime. I ran out of space on the back of the page, handed in my responses after the others and was told to return the next morning.

The process of selecting the jury began when the judge read out twelve names and two alternates. He explained that under the Constitution individuals are presumed innocent unless proven guilty, and he warned us not to talk among ourselves or to others until the trial was completed. Then, he asked the first juror to take the witness box and inquired about his background, whether he had family or acquaintances in the judicial system, knew the defendant, or had ever been convicted or arrested. A surprising number of jurors had uncles or cousins in the police force; more interesting were the stories about arrests for possession of drugs or driving while under the influence of alcohol. One man had been subjected to a brutal false arrest in a different state; three women—breaking into sobs—spoke about their children now in jail but said the convictions were justified. All stated that their encounters with the law would not influence their judgment in this case; and as their verbal proclamations were accepted, all were empaneled. For many potential jurors, the most difficult question turned on explaining the difference between the constitutional presumption of innocence and reaching a verdict of not guilty. Everyone said she or he understood the distinction between not being proven guilty and proving innocence, but the responses of two jurors were so contorted the judge dismissed them.

When the defense lawyer and the prosecutor posed their questions, my attention quickened. The defense attorney talked with each juror about constitutional rights to the presumption of innocence, to ask for a jury trial, and to have guilt proven beyond a reasonable doubt. Such rights, he suggested, were born in reaction to our past under colonial and oppressive governments. But his main purpose seemed to be to educate the jurors about their courtroom task. I wondered about his success when he said that the defendant—presumed innocent—did not need to speak in his own defense; many jurors agreed, stating that they also found it difficult to speak in public.

The defense lawyer implied that his client was accused of intentional but not premeditated murder, and the case involved drugs and an altercation about private property as well as a violent death. Hindsight is perfect, he said, but sometimes we take actions in defense of ourselves and property that have unintended consequences—and he presented personal tales about innocent intentions that led to unfortunate consequences. Would the juror, he asked, be offended by graphic pictures of a violent death, could she or he reach a judgment based solely on the facts of the case? Some potential jurors admitted to averting their eyes during violent TV episodes, others disapproved of drugs, but all said they could reach an independent decision based on the facts—except for one woman who admitted that she was influenced by the people around her. The judge promptly dismissed her while I admired her integrity and recalled the Solomon Asch experiments. When the court went into recess at noon, and we were told to return Monday morning, I was glad for the extra time and attended to other things over the weekend. But I felt that my sense of citizenship and national identity might not fit their expectations.

On Monday I was soon in the witness box, for several jurors were dismissed on account of their pressing business commitments. The judge asked how I wished to be addressed—Professor, Doctor, Mr.—and if I had problems fulfilling what could be a lengthy duty. Missing classes, he said, was not an adequate reason to be excused, so when his questions concerning my understanding of our constitutional rights were answered, the defense lawyer began, asking if I had any thoughts about questions he had posed.

I had a number of responses to choose among: our drug laws, why rural Latin American farmers might grow the product, the meaning of unanticipated consequences, and his supposition that individuals have private intentions. But I began with violence not because graphic photographs of the deceased might influence my decision, but because it was a complex topic. Violence was really a monopoly of the state, I suggested. Sometimes we were authorized by the state to commit violence in war but even that might be ambiguous. We all thought World War II was a "good" war, however many had doubts about Vietnam. I am not a pacifist, I stated, but I felt that violence was a failure, because it indicated a breakdown in communication. We have stopped the human conversation. I added that I had even co-written a book with "conversation" in the title, and as an anthropologist had spent my career fostering communications between different cultures. So, I found violence hard to excuse.

I knew, however, that he was talking about violence in defense of self and property, yet I found it even more problematic to justify. I said that I could see myself losing control and committing violence to defend my daughters and wife if they were threatened, but I was uncertain that I would be violent in defense of myself; it would not accomplish anything, and a nonviolent response would set a moral example for others. I also found difficulty with his suggestion that one could commit violence in defense of private property. Many of our individual constitutional rights, I suggested, had their origin in Locke's *Two Treatises* (1689), but I did not believe in his theory of private property, according to which individuals annex nature through the work they put into it. The theory assumes an initial division between humans and nature, and that personal labor creates value, giving individuals rights to the embodiment of their work. I did not believe in a labor theory of value nor in its extension to private property. Locke himself had exemplified the theory by using the image of an empty New World that Europeans had appropriated through their efforts. To the contrary, the Americas were densely populated at the conquest, and property was accorded by communities.

But, interjected the defense lawyer, you would judge the case on the facts presented? The word facts, I responded, also troubled me. Facts were not given but constructed, and so I preferred the word evidence as presented in a story. He agreed that evidence was the right word.

By now the prosecution, defense, and judge wanted to talk among themselves, and I could hear my dismissal being discussed at a sidebar. The judge told the others, "Let me try some more with him." Turning to me, he observed that I had lived in England. Have you ever played or watched rugby or polo, he asked? I told him that I had played a considerable amount of rugby at Cambridge.

"Let's take polo, then. It is an odd game, with lots of funny rules. But if you want to play, you have to play by the rules."

I agreed and recalled aloud the example of Socrates who drank hemlock; however, I said I was being honest in my answers.

But now, the accused's lawyer, grasping the implications of my view for his central argument, jumped to his feet and said, "Do you mean you think violence in defense of private property is not justified?"

"Absolutely not," I responded—and the judge raised his arm, pointed with his thumb, and told me to leave.

When I emerged from the courthouse, the sun was gleaming. Feeling relieved of questions about being an insider or outsider to the legal system, the foundations of identity and other postmodern terrors, I headed for lunch and the university.

A month later I saw one of the jurors, and she said the others waiting clapped for me after I left. Still later, I found a report of the trial in the newspaper.

> A Minneapolis man who said he snapped after a crack-cocaine deal and hit the seller on the head with a stick was found guilty Friday of second-degree murder . . . Thomas apparently thought he'd been sold some bad crack . . . Hare's fatal head injuries were described as so severe that they were consistent with those from a high-speed car crash. The prosecutor said the "stick" Thomas used was a 6- to 10-inch log . . . Thomas's attorney told the jury, "There is no proof that Mr. Thomas intended to take the life of a man he considered his friend, who he played chess with." The argument just escalated to the point that

> Thomas lashed out in a sudden, impassioned act, the defense attorney said. (*Minneapolis Star Tribune*, 9 May 1998, page B3; see also Gudeman 1998)

***

I had undertaken two long stretches of fieldwork, each time starting with a broad scope and narrowing it during the research. With increased academic obligations and an important home life, I needed to do shorter periods of fieldwork, and I wanted to move the inquiry closer to markets. In reverse of my prior method, I decided to start with a theme and let the form of fieldwork follow. Two topics had long caught my attention: the origin, idea, and presence of profit and socialism.

The Panamanian peasants told me that they never made a profit in agriculture, although the sugarcane mills did. In Colombia, the rural people said they made a profit only when they were raising crops for cash, and that endeavor had to be supported by growing food for their own consumption. In Mexico, survival in the Tzeltal village where I lived was so harsh that the idea of profitmaking never arose. Through these years, I had tried to follow the origin of the idea of profit from Aristotle through Turgot, Ricardo, Marx, and others. Now, my childhood and the field experiences offered a different clue to the way profit is created: making do. In the house economies I had studied, local creativity provided improvements in everyday living, although they did not yield a profit because nothing was sold. Starting with the idea of making do, however, I was led to Joseph Schumpeter's early writing on the way profit emerges from innovation. Could I find this blurry border between making do in the house and making a profit by innovation when a house economy enters the market? Alberto, my research partner in Colombia, had moved to Guatemala to raise his family, so I contacted him to see if he knew of promising examples there. He was interested in the topic as he was building a house-business and joined me in the research.

Off the main road leading west from Guatemala City, we spotted a brick maker who lived in an area that had accessible clay for mixing, molding, and firing bricks. Others near him also were making bricks, but he had a much larger and taller furnace for baking the clay. We stopped, approached and asked about his oven and chimney. He was delighted by our interest and with eyes lighting up told us that he had seen how iron rods were used to reinforce cement pillars in tall city buildings. "Why not," he asked himself, "lay the rods crosswise at the base of a very large oven to give it stability for a larger and taller chimney?" He planned the furnace in his head, and added "I could not sleep at night, because I was picturing it." The key to his innovation was the application of an idea from one domain (building walls) to another (a floor), which is the stuff of metaphoric thinking.

By the time we talked with him, he was beginning to produce bricks in his new huge oven. "My cost per brick is lower and the volume is increasing, but others are coming to see how it is done." Competition from others over time would erode his profit, he knew, but proud of his accomplishment he told us what he had done.

In a Guatemala City market, we watched men making tin utensils for household use. They bought sheets of tin and used simple tools for bending and shaping vessels for drinking, eating, watering, and other domestic uses. They worked alone.

As we wandered about the area, we found a tinsmith shop with three men, a father and his two sons. The father had organized the family into a production line. He cut the metal for a vessel, threw it to one son at the next table who began the shaping, who threw it to the other son for finishing the item. They took orders in the morning, did batch production, and were producing by day's end five to ten times more vessels than other tinsmiths. They had a higher profit as well, the sons earned more money than other workers, and the family had a television in every room of their house.

Smiling as he told us, the father explained, "I saw production lines in a factory and decided to adapt their division of labor for tin making." To keep competitors from copying his operation, he did not allow others to enter and watch his manufacturing process, although he permitted us to see what he was doing as well as witness his contagious energy. Like the brick maker, he was as energized by creating an enterprise as he was by the prospect of making more money.

Innovations may look rational in retrospect, because the profitable ones work, but they cannot be explained by rational choice. Information flows among people—whether seeing tall buildings in a city reinforced by iron struts or a long production line—can lead to new ideas just as objects themselves may suggest new uses. At first, I labeled this activity "art" to distinguish it from rational choice, because it seemed close to what Diderot (1751) meant by "Art" and something more than what Veblen (1922) called "Workmanship."

But these words do not capture the creative capacity I had seen in Panama and Colombia, because "innovations" occur in everyday life. In Colombia, I saw peasants fashion rain gear from discarded plastic, and in Panama cast-off tins for marketable grains became household containers. In the Guatemala countryside, an inverted porcelain bowl was strung by wires above a chimney to prevent rain from falling onto the cooking fire. In a Guatemala market, however, sandals for sale were fashioned from abandoned automobile tires. If first practiced in the house economy as a way to be thrifty, making do can also lead to innovations in markets that yield a profit.

***

I had long wondered if there was a similarity between the house economy and socialism, for during my research on the history of the house economy I came across some striking phrases written by James Steuart in 1767:

> Oeconomy, in general, is the art of providing for all the wants of a family, with prudence and frugality. The object of it in a family, is therefore to provide for the nourishment, the other wants, and the employment of every individual.
>
> What economy is in a family, political oeconomy is in a state . . .
>
> The principal object of this science is to secure a certain fund of subsistence for all the inhabitants . . .
>
> It is the business of a statesman to judge of the expediency of different schemes of oeconomy, and by degrees to model the minds of his subjects. ([1767] 1966: 15–17)

Steuart projected the image of the house economy to the state and monarchy. In both, work is for a group, incentives and rewards are partly social, and planning is centralized or cooperative. I had journeyed from the almost isolated house economy in Mexico and the highlands of Colombia, to the subsistence and cash cropping house economy in Panama, to the house-business in Guatemala. I saw ways the house economy is involved in modes of transactions from gifting, to labor exchange, to the use of money. Would any of these findings about the house economy be useful in the context of socialism? I needed to see Cuba.

The island had intrigued me since my Panama study of sugarcane. The manager of the Panama sugar mill, with whom I spent time, had come from Cuba after the revolution. Cuba had been the sugarcane leader in production per hectare, but Panama's sugar production and productivity had been increasing in response to the United States prohibition on the import of Cuban sugar after the revolution. What was the situation now?

Cubans were using two currencies: the Cuban peso and the dollar (the peso was worth $0.04 on the unofficial black market). I wondered how the two moneys were used in a single economy, especially given the fraught relations between the island and the United States. Cuba and the United States did not trade, and even if Cubans used the dollar in ordinary exchanges, the peso had no value in the United States. From where did the dollars come, how were they used with pesos in Cuba, and what happened to them?

Alberto had taken several groups of Latin American students to Cuba, so I contacted him and we met on the island. Cuba, however, was off limits for Americans. Entry was possible for United States citizens but the US government watched reentry to the United States, and stories of prosecution circulated. I secured written permission from the University of Minnesota for the research and flew through Central America, wearing a money belt stuffed with dollars because there were no ATMs in Cuba.

I used dollars everywhere and converted less than $10.00 to Cuban pesos, which I used for rides in the collective taxis that circulated in Havana. Dollars were the preferred currency for everything else, whether lodging, food, books, or cigars. I was surprised dollars were readily accepted until I learned how the government managed the dual money economy.

I especially wanted to see how state control of the economy worked at the local level and had my first exposure when we stayed in a house rather than a tourist hotel, as householders are allowed to register and rent rooms to visitors. The government calculates how much a house will make and taxes it a fixed amount each month. Our residence had three extra rooms but the owner was paying to rent only one. One evening on returning to the house, I could not find my backpack.

"What happened to my backpack?" I asked the proprietress.

"It is under your bed," she said.

"Huh?"

"We are allowed to rent only one room. If the inspector finds more people here, I lose my license," she added, because she would be turning her home into an independent business. Later, she explained that house inspectors had to be changed every three months. The first time the inspector arrived he collected the official tariff for renting a room. The next time the owner and inspector forged a personal relation. The third time the inspector was paid not to report infractions, so inspectors were rotated every quarter. Apocryphal or true, the story provided my first insight into the way socialist regulation of the economy can be undermined.

When Russian support of Cuba evaporated in the early 1990s, some market activity was permitted on the island to keep the economy running, and both house and one-person enterprises had emerged in many corners of the economy, such as restaurants, room rentals for tourists, auto repair shops, knife sharpeners, fruit and vegetable sellers, and electricians. Because I had looked at the house-business in which labor is house supplied, I talked to Cubans about their small businesses. No wages are paid to working family members, for that would be illegal as it would represent a capital-labor relationship.

The small-scale sellers make do. Old cigarette lighters are refilled with fluid for sale. The 1950s cars from the United States are repaired in the street to serve as collective taxis. Making do now was a response not only to lack of personal purchasing power but also to national scarcity.

I understood Cuba's dual currency system when I learned how Cuba is helped by dollars from Miami and tourism. The Miami remittances amounted to $250 million per year, which is about $25.00 per person annually. In comparison, official salaries were $8.00–$12.00 per month, so the Miami money added 25 percent to the normal wage. It seemed ironic that Miami Cubans are supporting their families in Cuba while opposing the system under which many of them still chose to live.

Tourism in the restored Old Havana and the beach hotels also brought in dollars. This influx of people with money spawned trade and employment from small services, to prostitution, to the illegal sale of cigars. One woman working in a cigar factory explained, when she sold me a large quantity of cigars, that at work she received two boxes of cigars a month from the enterprise in addition to a daily meal and a small salary. She kept the job because she stole boxes of cigars (by paying off the factory inspector) and sold a box of them on the black market to tourists, such as myself, for $30.00, which was far larger than her legal earnings. On the international market the same cigars brought $600.00.

State enterprises provide their workers with more than a salary—cigars, harvest products, a large midday meal—but pinching from the government seemed rife. One diehard communist said he stole a car from the government, and I heard other accounts of pilferage ranging from trucks to bean harvests and was shown how to rig a telephone to someone else's line to avoid paying the government fee.

The legal economy drew my attention as a shifting mix of socialism and controlled markets. The consumer side was exhibited in the types of stores. Every citizen receives a coupon or ration book entitling him or her to purchase a small quantity of basics at a local store. The goods include rice, cooking oil, salt, soap, potatoes, and beans, all at low prices. A pound of salt cost 35 centavos or a little more than one US penny, but the quantities are rationed. A family can purchase one bar of soap each month, and the soap on offer alternates each month between hand and laundry soap. The rations last about one-third of a month.

The ration system that reaches people through small outlets with equal distribution represents socialism in practice. Like the house economy in Panama and Colombia that depends on a base accumulated and held to support basic living, the Cuban ration system provides the base for the entire economy, again as if the house economy were projected to the nation.

The market side of the economy is controlled and seemed to grow and diminish with political decisions. Produce markets, covered by a roof and open on the sides, contain both private and state stalls that sell vegetables, rice, tubers, greens, and some hog meat. Prices are about ten times higher than in the ration stores, the quality is better, the range of goods is broader, and the quantity available is larger.

State and cooperative farms that exceed their quotas, which are delivered to the state for its enterprises for feeding their workers and for distribution to the ration stores, sell their extra amounts to the market vendors. The state-operated vendors offer less costly, lower quality goods than the private ones, which sets a ceiling on the prices charged at the private stalls. As in the microenterprises, the private stalls cannot hire workers because that would lead to the exploitation of laborers by owners.

The food markets, which supplement the ration stores, were crowded in the morning when people purchased their daily sustenance. Watching Cubans use both dollars and pesos for their purchases, I was puzzled again by use of the two currencies. If dollars enter the economy by remittances from the United States and tourism, why do they not keep growing in volume and swamp Cuban pesos? The puzzle was solved when I saw a third type of store that fascinated me for its innovativeness. Called Stores for Regaining Foreign Exchange, they sell imported goods for purchase in dollars.

A mini-mall had opened in Havana with fifty stores selling imported goods, such as hair care products, butter, liquor, hardware, frozen foods, and furniture, all of which are owned by the government. It uses the dollars received in these stores to purchase goods from New Zealand, Australia, Canada, Denmark, Spain and elsewhere, except the United States. The entire mall was slightly larger than a department store in a United States mall.

Now I understood how the two-currency system operates. Using dollars and foreign currency the government purchases goods for the mall and sells them at a higher price. The returns buy more goods for sale and national supplies, including food for the ration system. Soaking up US money from Miami and tourism that circulates in Cuba and using it for external purchases that are sold internally or distributed by central planning, the dollar system helps the economy stay afloat.

By inserting an island of market exchange within socialism, I thought the dollar retrieval system might pose a threat to socialist practices and create a tension within the Cuban economy, but seeing it solved my mental puzzle about how a dual currency system operates.

***

Alberto and I hired a taxi for several days, which was illegal as the owner was not licensed to carry more than one person when traveling outside the city. We drove east from Havana to see the sugarcane fields. When I undertook the Panama fieldwork in 1966–67, Cuba was the productivity leader in sugarcane. The Panamanian peasants raised about 20–25 tons of sugarcane per hectare. Cuba at that time secured yields reaching 80–90 tons per hectare, but now Cuban productivity had dropped to 40–70 tons per hectare, and some fields were not being used. The mills still bore names like "George Washington" and had not been reconditioned after the revolution, although the industry employs 400,000 workers during the harvest.

Spying four workers in an old sugarcane field, we stopped to watch them harvest pineapples. One man was selecting and cutting each pineapple with a machete. He dropped it into a wheelbarrow pushed by a second man, while the third rested at the end of the row. A woman stood apart, did not talk with the men, and carried a clipboard on which she recorded how many pineapples were picked and how many were left on a plant. The crop was sent to the tourist hotels. I was observing labor-intensive production with socialist monitoring.

Government surveillance seemed necessary, because evasion was more rampant than I imagined and state resources sometimes were turned to private use. Farmers quietly explained that they privately sold part of a harvest earmarked for the government. One man sold pizza from his house that had no employees and legally bought some of the ingredients from government suppliers, but he had also made friends with suppliers who diverted the ingredients to him for cash, and he fabricated his receipts for government inspectors, because with his wife's help, he sold many more pizzas than allowed. We visited him at his house where he showed us how he rigged his electric line to his neighbor's to avoid the cost of installing electricity.

The state seemed to monitor everything. In market terms the watchdogs were an overhead cost, but markets use accounting systems and the stimulus of profit to motivate behavior, and from that perspective, socialism is inefficient in the allocation of resources and labor.

I was sorry to see this moral breakdown, but in Havana I bought cigars from the woman who held a job in a cigar factory and pilfered some of the product. The cigars were the same classic brand (Cohiba) that Fidel smoked and that I found in President Kennedy's dining room at Hyannis Port years before. To evade United States customs and disguise where I had been, I hid the purchase in my shoes that were stowed in a suitcase. Unlike the Colombian coffee that was legal and lost, I ended the Cuba research with this illegal product and savored the idea that my earlier work helped me understand Cuba.

***

In the autumn of 2002, Roxane and I headed to the Swedish Collegium for Advanced Study in Uppsala where she shared my office, joined the group for lunch, and participated in the seminars. By now, I had been drawn to the idea of risk. In Panama and Colombia, the peasants address risk in agriculture by diversifying their crops and seed type, and use words such as luck, chance, and fortune to talk about unpredictable outcomes. In contrast, on Wall Street and in the financial sphere of economy, newly developed tools addressing risk were statistical and applied across a range of transactions.

In this developing sphere of finance, new tools, such as derivatives, are deployed. A derivative is a way of buying and selling risk, which is to say transferring a risk to someone else through the exchange of money, which is something the peasants were not able to do. In the language I use, a derivative is "the price of a price" or in expanded language, it is the cost of insuring against a risky price over time, just as capitalist farmers try to assure the value of their harvest against unpredictable grain prices through crop insurance purchased in advance. A derivative, however, focuses not on the price of a tangible asset, such as a farmer's wheat or corn, but on a price and its variance. I was fascinated by this new tool, because it had little to do with the tangible economies that I knew, but might ultimately influence them. I thought of this new realm as meta-finance or the finance of finance as it had to do with the pricing of variations in a price.

This new sphere introduced a new type of risk—a financial one—and in a footnote to a book that emerged from the Swedish stay and written before the 2008 crisis that was partly caused by the new tools erupted, I wrote of the risk of using statistical analyses of risk based on numerically short historical trajectories, because they are not a true sample of the possibilities, unlike the farmer who has generations of experience raising crops. I should have underlined the warning, because that is what soon happened. I had been drawn again to the economics side of my mentality, but it helped me understand better what the peasants in Panama and Colombia had been doing (Gudeman 2008).

***

In 1999, the Max Planck Institute for Social Anthropology was established in Halle, Germany, and is part of the Max Planck Society funded by the German government. When the Institute moved to its permanent quarters in 2005, it held a conference of anthropologists and historians, and one of the two directors, Chris Hann, asked me to give the summary presentation. I had met him twenty years earlier in Cambridge, England, but we had had no contact in the interval. After succeeding conferences, Hann asked if I would direct with him a research project consisting of post PhD students who would be supported by the Institute.

Comparative work, centered on a common theme, had once been popular in anthropology, but for more than fifty years anthropologists had primarily undertaken solitary fieldwork in disparate sites. Comparative work, I felt, would help link anthropology to the other social sciences, and having learned the value of joint work in Colombia, a focused team project I thought could yield a stronger result. Working in a different culture area of the world but rural zones on the edges of markets yet in the context of postsocialism was attractive in light of my prior field experiences.

The Institute supported our team of six postdoctoral researchers for three and a half years. The members had worked in and would return to Hungary, Romania, Moldova, Macedonia, Bulgaria, and Kyrgyzstan. The project started in 2009 and carried on until 2012. I lived in Halle for two and a half years, and Roxane was there most of the time and shared my office.

We labeled the project Economy and Ritual and soon added a second project focused on house economy. When the researchers undertook fieldwork, they also found examples of the godparenthood system, my early interest in Panama, and it became a subfocus for several members.

Roxane traveled with me to a Bulgarian village, high in the southern Rhodope Mountains where one of our team was located.[1] Bulgaria had suffered economically after the fall of the Soviet Union and the collapse of central planning. Western optimists expected markets to suddenly emerge, spurred through "shock therapy," but that did not happen. After the breakup of the Soviet Union and the disappearance of socialism, farmers and others in the Rhodopes initially bartered locally with prices set in potatoes that were a central part of the diet. I felt at home with this food that originated in the mountains of South America, with the near presence of barter, and with the emergence of the house as an important production, consumption, and storage unit. In one house I found a large pile of potatoes stored in the basement, much as I had seen in Colombia years before.

Referring to the house, people in the Rhodopes spoke of "working in a closed circle." The metaphor indicates that all members contribute to its survival, which is similar to what I observed in Panama and Colombia. Some house members worked outside the village, some raised a few crops and animals for home consumption, and some fashioned a few items at home, such as slippers and clothes. Working in a closed circle meant pooling the returns and using market relations in relation to house resources and sustenance. The language and local environment were different from Latin America, but the similarity of the house as a central economic institution in these different parts of the world was remarkable.

Roxane and I stayed in a small village in Hungary.[2] The land surrounding the village had been held by the state and its cultivation had provided local employment through state cooperatives. Now, the land was farmed by outside enterprises, and with increased mechanization and collapse of the state farms, agricultural jobs in the village had disappeared. A number of the villagers survived on welfare or impermanent work for the state. In this area the house and community had emerged as the central economic institutions given their weak integration in the new market economy similar to what I had observed in Latin America.

In Macedonia, green leaves of tobacco were drying on racks, exactly as I had seen and helped prepare in rural Colombia, but the racks were in sheds opening to the street, and it was primarily women who were stringing up the tobacco during the day. In northern Colombia a group of males and females gathered in the evening under an open thatch porch to string tobacco and talk. If there were small differences in the way the tobacco was prepared for sale, there were larger similarities in the people's relation to the market. In northern Colombia, the small tobacco growers were the first to feel the effects of changes in the world market. When world tobacco sales fell, their crop was not bought. In the Macedonian village, the tobacco farmers encountered a low demand problem for a different reason: their product was not yet accepted by the European Union. I was again at the economic margin of tobacco growing and seeing the effects of market power and dependence.[3]

The researchers found house economies, rituals, cash cropping, and godparenthood patterns that were recognizable if slightly different from what I knew in Latin America.[4]

***

For more than half a century, my journey took me through a collection of economies that may be viewed as a square with the house in the center. In Mexico, I lived with farmers who could hardly raise enough food to support their households. In Panama and Colombia, my focus had been the house economy at the edge of a market economy. In Guatemala, I explored the small house-business that had a limited connection to the market economy. In Cuba, I was able to see socialism and central planning as it influenced and relied on the house economy, and in Eastern Europe, I saw the rise in importance of the house economy after the collapse of socialism and the slow emergence of a market economy. The details, ethnography, language, and rituals of economy were different in each place but familiar, and I was stimulated to think again about the historical connections between Europe and the areas I studied, which was the puzzle I initially encountered in the study of godparenthood with its variations through history and across continents: similar practices with local distinctions.

Market economies develop increasingly abstract spheres of exchange that reap increasing returns. They are gained from the everyday sphere, as in Panama and Colombia where measurements are made by paces, arms, and baskets to help provide sustenance for the house often supplemented by cash cropping, to small-scale commerce as in Guatemala, to the financial domain as on Wall Street, where statistical measurements of risk and asset allocation are deployed that amass financial capital (Gudeman 2016).

The concept of rent, an unearned receipt, includes any taking above what labor receives for its efforts, whether it is locally classified as profit, interest, tribute, or another levy. Considering all my field studies, rents flow from the material environment to the house economy, to larger communities, to commercial exchange such as stores that make a profit, to the banking sphere that provides loans at interest, and then to the financial sphere of risk calculation and asset allocation, such as hedge funds that gather an unearned return on capital. The flows of rent connect the material world to the mathematical spheres of economy. Rent recipients, to adapt a phrase from market economists, are "free riders," an expression I like because it reminds me of the trams in Germany where passengers pay for their rides on the honor system, while rent recipients do not. The various patterns of securing rent provide a comparative way of viewing the economies where I have lived from the United States, to Mexico, Panama, Colombia, Guatemala, Cuba, and Eastern Europe.

In the latter part of the twentieth century and the following one, by application of innovations based on the statistics of risk and asset allocation, which have brought extraordinary returns to financial centers in the world, the unequal distribution of wealth as wages and rents, in the United States and spreading through the world, has grown on a scale never before witnessed. My journey thus concludes with the unanswered question that I posed to my father in the Midwest of the United States many years ago: "Where does it end?"

## Notes

1. We visited Detelina Tocheva who had established warm relations with villagers, kindly escorted us in the area, and provided us with information about the village.
2. We were hosted by Bea Vidacs, another member of the research team, who provided the ethnographic information.
3. In Macedonia, the entire team was hosted by Miladina Monova who provided this information.
4. The research team included Jennifer Cash, Nathan Light, Miladina Monova, Detelina Tocheva, Monica Vasile, and Bea Vidacs. Our comparative work was published in two books: *Economy and Ritual: Studies of Postsocialist Transformations* (2015); and *Oikos and Market: Explorations in Self-Sufficiency after Socialism* (2015).

# References

Bartlett, Charles. 1967. "One Man's Key to Latin Success." *Boston Globe*, 29 April, 13.

Diderot, Denis. 1751. "Art." *Encyclopédie, ou Dictionnaire Raisonné des Sciences des Arts et des Métiers*, ed. Denis Diderot and Jean Le Rond d'Alembert, 1, 713–17. Paris: Briasson, David, Le Breton, Durand.

Georgescu-Roegen, Nicolas. 1971. *The Entropy Law and the Economic Process*. Cambridge, MA: Harvard University Press.

Gudeman, Stephen. 1972. "The Compadrazgo as a Reflection of the Natural and Spiritual Person." (The Curl Prize Essay 1971). *Proceedings of the Royal Anthropological Institute for 1971*: 45–71. https://doi.org/10.2307/3031761.

——. 1978. *The Demise of a Rural Economy*. London: Routledge & Kegan Paul.

——. 1998. "The Juror." *Anthropology Today* 14(5): 15–16.

——. 2008. *Economy's Tension: The Dialectics of Community and Market*. New York: Berghahn Books.

——. 2016. *Anthropology and Economy*. Cambridge: Cambridge University Press.

Gudeman, Stephen, and Alberto Rivera. 1990. *Conversations in Colombia: The Domestic Economy in Life and Text*. Cambridge: Cambridge University Press.

Gudeman, Stephen, and Chris Hann, eds. 2015. *Economy and Ritual: Studies of Postsocialist Transformations*. New York: Berghahn.

——. eds. 2015. *Oikos and Market: Explorations in Self-Sufficiency after Socialism*. New York: Berghahn.

Keynes, John Maynard. 1924. "Alfred Marshall, 1842–1924." *The Economic Journal* 34(135): 311–72.

——. [1936] 2017. *The General Theory of Employment, Interest and Money*. London: Routledge.

Lévi-Strauss, Claude. 1962. *The Savage Mind*. London: Weidenfeld and Nicolson.

Locke, John. 1689. *The Two Treatises of Civil Government*, ed. John Hollis. Indianapolis: Liberty Fund.

Malinowski, Bronislaw. [1922] 1961. *Argonauts of the Western Pacific*. New York. Dutton.

Mauss, Marcel. [1925] 2016. *The Gift*, trans. Jane I. Guyer. Chicago: Hau Books.

Polanyi, Karl. 1944. *The Great Transformation*. New York: Dutton.

——. 1968. *Primitive, Archaic and Modern Economies*, ed. George Dalton. Garden City, NY: Anchor Books.

Rappaport, Roy. 1978. *Pigs for the Ancestors*. New Haven, CT: Yale University Press.

Ricardo, David. 1815. *An Essay on the Influence of Corn on the Profits of Stock*. London: John Murray.

——. 1951–52. *The Works and Correspondence of David Ricardo*, ed. Piero Sraffa, vol. IV. Cambridge: Cambridge University Press.

Rostow, Walt. 1960. *The Stages of Economic Growth: A Non-Communist Manifesto*. Cambridge: Cambridge University Press.

Sraffa, Piero. 1960. *Production of Commodities by Means of Commodities*. Cambridge: Cambridge University Press.

Steuart, James. [1767] 1966. *An Inquiry into the Principles of Political Oeconomy*, ed. Andrew S. Skinner. Chicago: University of Chicago Press.

Veblen, Thorstein. 1922. *The Instinct of Workmanship*. New York: B. W. Huebsch.

——. 1942. *The Place of Science in Modern Civilisation and Other Essays*. New York: Viking Press.

——. [1904] 1978. *The Theory of Business Enterprise*. Transaction Books: New Brunswick.

——. [1899] 1979. *The Theory of the Leisure Class*. Penguin Books: Harmondsworth.

# Index

www.ingramcontent.com/pod-product-compliance
Lightning Source LLC
Chambersburg PA
CBHW070936030426
42336CB00014BA/2700

* 9 7 8 1 8 0 0 7 3 6 0 6 1 *